christian
educators' guide
to evaluating
and developing
curriculum

christian educators' guide
to evaluating and developing curriculum

NANCY FERGUSON
Foreword by Marlene LeFever

JUDSON PRESS
PUBLISHERS SINCE 1824
VALLEY FORGE, PA

Christian Educators' Guide to Evaluating and Developing Curriculum
© 2008 by Judson Press, Valley Forge, PA 19482-0851
All rights reserved.

Library of Congress Cataloging-in-Publication Data

Ferguson, Nancy.
   Christian educators' guide to evaluating and developing curriculum / Nancy Ferguson.
      p. cm.
   ISBN-13: 978-0-8170-1523-7 (pbk. : alk. paper) 1. Christian education—Curricula—Evalu-
ation. 2. Curriculum planning. I. Title.

   BV1471.3.F47 2007
   268—dc22

                                                           2007042257

Printed on recycled paper in the U.S.A.

First Edition, 2008.

To the churches, teachers, students,
writers, and curriculum editors
who have challenged me and taught me
everything I know about curriculum.

You know who you are!

Contents

PART 3 Writing Curriculum Resources

PART 4 Adapting Curriculum Resources

Foreword

When I was a teacher in a missionary school in Japan, I fell in love with curriculum resources, or more to the point, I fell in love with what curriculum materials could do in the lives of students. I taught Bible to seventh and eighth graders, and almost to a child, they hated the subject. The textbook I had inherited was filled with no-brainer questions, such as "Who are the two disciples mentioned in verse 7?" No pictures! Nothing creative at all. Even the cover was gray. The third day of class I passed the waste basket and told the kids to throw their textbooks into it. They were delighted, and I was too new a teacher to think of what the repercussions might be. Suddenly with no books, I found myself writing curriculum materials, often staying no more than two or three days ahead of the kids. It was exhausting, challenging, and totally fun. There were actually some days that, when the bell rang to end class, students did not want to leave. I lived for those days! (By the way, I didn't really throw the books away. After class, I dug them out of the waste basket and hid them under piles of stuff in a closet. I hope that to this day no one has found them.)

Nancy Ferguson knows what goes into choosing or writing the right curriculum resources for different churches with unique needs. Her book guides leaders through both processes—choosing or writing—in a step-by-step way that feels easy and seamless. I wish I had had this book when I was struggling with my self-imposed curriculum writing. Studying our Creator's book should never be boring. If a church follows Nancy's guidelines, their curriculum materials will meet the needs of that particular church. The resources, be they purchased or written, will feel right!

I particularly like Nancy's six key elements that become building blocks for evaluating and writing curriculum resources. They work. Those same elements can also help a pastor more perfectly target the sermon to the congregation, or help a college or seminary professor guide students in their first curriculum evaluation or development experiences.

Choosing effective curriculum resources is not just one of the things Christian educators have in their job descriptions. It's the most important thing. Good curriculum materials in the hands of trained volunteers can, with the help of the Holy Spirit, become the catalyst for discipleship growth for students of all ages. Recently David C. Cook completed a landmark study in Christian education. Teachers identified real-life transformation as their highest goal in teaching. What is included in transformation? Bible knowledge, a Christian worldview, life change, and participation in spiritual disciplines, Christian growth, missional activities, and active worship. In Eugene Peterson's paraphrase of Colossians, Paul defines transformation poetically: "I want you woven into a tapestry of love, in touch with everything there is to know of God. Then you will have a mind confident and at rest, focused on Christ" (THE MESSAGE).

If you're ready for the adventure of writing your own curriculum resources, this Christian Educators' Guide is an invaluable tool. This second half of the book may be the most used portion. Sixty-one percent of all Sunday school teachers are not teaching exactly what's in the book. Eighty percent of paid professionals are writing or customizing their own curriculum. David C. Cook's landmark study asked why teachers were willing to go to all this work. Children's leaders gave as their three top reasons: dissatisfaction with existing materials (36%), not enough Bible content (29%), and to save money (25%). Almost half of the youth leaders (47%) who write their own materials do it simply because they want to do it! Having a pattern to follow and Ferguson's training course to teach the pattern will make the creative process a whole lot more effective and a whole lot less frustrating.

I received a letter on a day when I was tired of teaching and all the work that goes with it—including curriculum resource development. I tore open the envelope and read: "Dear Marlene, You probably don't remember me, but years ago you were my Bible teacher. That was the year I decided I would give Jesus my life. I'm now a pastor's wife and a mother, but more important to you, I suspect, is that I'm also a Sunday school teacher." She had been in my class the year I threw away the boring texts. Suddenly, I wasn't tired anymore!

Marlene LeFever
Vice President of Educational Development
David C. Cook
Colorado Springs, Colorado

Preface

This is a book I have wanted to write for a long time. It is born out of my many experiences as a church educator, teacher, and curriculum writer and editor. I hope that it is a book that you have been seeking for an equally long time and that it will fill your need for a single sourcebook for both evaluating and writing curriculum materials.

As a Christian educator for both churches and judicatories, I am aware that churches have very few tools for evaluating curricula—printed and media resources for learning. Thus, Christian teachers often choose curriculum materials based on teacher helps and appearance, such as attractive student handouts. When I have taught seminary students, the lack of a textbook on curriculum theory and practice has hampered my teaching and their learning.

About fifteen years ago I stumbled into the role of curriculum writer when a friend asked me to revise materials for republication. Since then I have lost count of the number of hours I have logged developing lesson plans for publishing houses. Through that experience I have learned the importance of having an overall purpose statement for a curriculum series reinforced with clear goals and objectives for session plans.

I realized my work with curricula had come full circle when I was asked to become the editor for an ecumenical curriculum product to be used in church camps. This experience enabled me to gain a new view of the church-related publishing world and to shape a curriculum program from beginning to end. Composing the chapters on curriculum writing for this book has given me some new insights into how I train the writers for that curriculum.

I want to add a brief note here about the use of the word *curriculum* in this book. There are a variety of definitions for the word, such as those given by *The American Heritage Dictionary* as "All the courses of study offered by an educational institution" or "A group of related courses, often in a special field of study." I hope you will keep these broader definitions in mind when you consider the question of evaluating or developing curriculum resources for your congregation. Properly speaking, curriculum refers to your entire Christian education program and not merely to the printed resources you may purchase or write to accomplish your educational goals. For that reason, this book starts by leading you through a process of discernment—to consider what your vision is for Christian education and discipleship and what strategies you want to employ in implementing that vision. Only with an understanding of the overarching *curriculum* can you effectively evaluate existing resources or develop your own materials.

Throughout this volume, I will strive to maintain this distinction—referring to the printed or media curriculum tools as curriculum resources or materials. However, for the sake of expediency, I may also fall back on the more colloquial use of the term *curriculum* as an abbreviated reference to those resources—the books and booklets, take-home papers, DVDs, and online resources that are used primarily for Christian education in the local church.

I want to express my appreciation to the people who played a part in the creation of this handbook. Thanks to Ann Knox, Pamela Mitchell-Legg, Nancy Fitzgerald, Norma Calvo-Cascante, Cindy Ruhl, and Kim Kemper who generously shared their time and expertise to read this manuscript as it was being written. Thanks to Rebecca Irwin-Diehl, my editor, for her patience with my questions and my requests for "just one more" extension. And a big thanks to Casey Williams for bringing Judson and me together.

It is my hope that this handbook will enrich the educational ministry of your congregation. I welcome conversations about curriculum and am available to train writers. You can contact me via my website at BlueTreeResources.org.

Nancy Ferguson
July 2007
Richmond, Virginia

Introduction

The shelves of religious bookstores are filled with curriculum resource choices. Catalogs for church school curricula litter Christian education offices, and church closets are stacked with old printed curricula that no one knows what to do with. Many churches are writing their own curriculum materials out of frustration with the choices available on the market. The question of which curriculum to use is never far away from the minds of educators and Christian education committees.

Once upon a time, teachers may have felt qualified to plan Bible lessons. Today's teachers, however, rarely have that confidence. Prepared resources—whether purchased or written by someone in the church—offer teachers a lesson structure, schedule suggestions, biblical background, and activity ideas. Very few people would agree to teach if prepared curriculum resources were not available!

Curriculum resources come in many forms today. The traditional leader book accompanied by student books or handouts is still available. But curriculum materials also come on CDs with resources that can be printed out or used by students on computer. Downloadable resources can be obtained from the Internet for a fee or at no charge. Many curriculum products are available on DVD to be watched in the classroom. Regardless of the form, many Christian educators consider the key to an effective Christian education program to be the "right" curriculum, one that has the following attributes:

- Easy for teachers to use

- Engaging to learners and keeps them coming back

- Craft kits

- Colorful

- Inexpensive

- Easy to order and return

- Contents match church's need

- Denominationally promoted

Some congregations also seek materials that are consistent with the educational goals of the congregation and/or reflective of the biblical and theological traditions of the church. Unfortunately, these criteria are sometimes considered less important in the search for curricula than are the other named qualities.

The desire for curriculum resources that excite, inspire, and involve learners is widespread. The level of frustration related to the search for "just the right" curriculum resources among both professional and lay educational leaders is high. The bad news is that the perfect curriculum product probably doesn't exist.

The good news, however, is that it is possible to provide curriculum materials for a congregation's educational ministry that are consistent with their understanding of what it means to be a Christian and of how Christian faith forms. That goal can be accomplished in one of two ways: educators can use clear guidelines for evaluation of purchased curriculum resources, or they can write curriculum resources that are in harmony with their beliefs.

Purpose of This Book

The purpose of this book is to help you identify, create, or adapt a printed curriculum that fits the beliefs and goals of your congregation. Through the processes and activities suggested in this handbook, you will be able to do the following:

- Articulate the goal and purpose of your congregation's educational ministry

- Identify the six key elements of your Christian education program

- Learn to use the six key elements to evaluate purchased curriculum resources

- Develop a scope and sequence for writing your own resources

- Write session plans that are in agreement with your six key elements

- Equip writers to develop session plans consistent with your educational purpose

- Train teachers to use the curriculum materials

- Evaluate the curriculum resources you have written

The first section of this book describes each aspect of a process that will enable you to reach your goal of providing a curriculum that is in harmony with your educational purposes—in other words, to ensure your curriculum resources are compatible with your overarching curriculum (see Preface for clarification of this distinction). All churches, regardless of whether they seek to evaluate purchased curriculum or to write their own resources, will need to identify the six key elements of the Christian education program outlined in part 1. Once these elements are named, a congregation can choose to follow the processes described in part 2 to evaluate curricula, to use the guidelines in part 3 to write their own curriculum, or to use the strategies in part 4 to adapt curriculum resources.

The first chapter of part 1 is designed to help congregations determine the purpose of their educational ministry. Three major areas are considered in the process of reaching a common sense of purpose. First, a congregation needs to examine some theological questions, most importantly what they believe about being a Christian and the methods they prefer to use for studying Scripture. Second, a congregation needs to consider what they believe about how faith is passed on through their educational ministry. These are the issues related to educational methods and practices. Finally, a congregation needs to identify the components of their present educational program. These are information questions.

In the second chapter of part 1 of this handbook are two workshop designs for educational committees to use in identifying the six key elements of their educational programs. As part of the process, your congregation will gather information about your current Christian education program—number of classes; number of children, youth, and adults enrolled; curriculum materials currently being used; and so on. Only after these six key elements are identified are you ready to consider the question of curriculum resources. At the conclusion of the two workshops, you and your committee will have the information needed to evaluate purchased resources or to write your own.

Six Key Elements

Key 1: Purpose or goal for Christian education in your church

Key 2: What the Bible is and how you use it in your educational ministry

Key 3: Settings for educational ministry in your congregation

Key 4: Content to be taught in your educational ministry

Key 5: Role of teachers in your educational ministry

Key 6: Role of learners in your educational ministry

Part 2 focuses on the evaluation of purchased curriculum resources. Often Christian education committees and/or teachers make choices regarding print resources based on ease of use and attractive covers rather than on how well the resources match the goals of Christian education in their church. Using the six key elements they have identified, an education committee can establish which curriculum will enable the congregation to reach the goal the committee has identified for its educational ministry.

A workshop format will assist those charged with choosing a curriculum to determine whether the goals and perspectives of a curriculum resource are consistent with their own six key elements. A cost assessment worksheet and a curriculum evaluation form are included to facilitate the comparison of different resources.

Part 3 provides guidelines for writing your own resources. It leads you through the process of identifying the content you want to include in the curriculum, the scope of that content and how it will be organized, and the themes for each session of the course.

The first chapter of part 3—"Get Ready"—begins with a consideration of whether writing your own curriculum is right for your church. It will also enable you to determine the content, scope, and arrangement of the content of the resources you want to write. As a final step you will determine the biblical passage for each theme.

In the next chapter—"Get Set"—you will learn how to develop a goal and objective for each session so that they will enable you to reach your congregational educational goals. You will create an outline for the individual sessions by applying the six key elements. Then you will use a Bible exploration process to examine the meaning, setting, and concepts of each biblical passage you have matched with the themes.

Finally, in "Go," I provide guidelines for writing. I also suggest elements for training writers and supply a workshop design. Among the topics included in this section are educational methods, writing techniques, learning styles, and brief descriptions of age group characteristics.

Throughout the chapters in part 3, I use a sample mission study for fourth and fifth graders to give you a specific example of each component of the curriculum writing process. As you learn about each step, the sample demonstrates how to do that step. At the end of the chapter, you will find a complete session plan.

The final section, part 4, includes some suggestions for how to adapt an existing curriculum. It assumes that churches will sometimes complete the identification of their six key elements and the evaluation of available curriculum materials only to find that there is no perfect match for their educational goals. They may conclude that they can adapt the closest match so that it *will* meet their needs.

Therefore, chapter 8 in this book introduces two major methods for adapting existing curriculum. One method adds information—such as biblical background, life application, creative arts activities, and additional questions—to the published curriculum resource. The second method includes additions to the curriculum as well as rearranging the order and creating new elements for a session plan. Congregations are encouraged to consider the time such adaptations require and whether the results make that investment worthwhile in terms of reaching the goals of their educational ministry.

How to Use This Book

As noted above, the book has four main sections. All congregations using the handbook should begin with the identification of the six key elements, because these key elements serve as the foundation for both the evaluation process and the writing guidelines.

Congregations will need to begin by agreeing to make a commitment to the time and energy required for the identification of the six key elements. The more people and the more interest groups within the church that can be involved in this process, the more representative of the congregation the results will be. While the church education committee can be the core group working through the process, parents, youth, and older adults should have a voice as well.

The first step in either evaluation or creation of curriculum resources is the use of the two workshop designs given in chapter 1. While this handbook is a source of good ideas for evaluating and creating curriculum, its main focus is the development and use of the key elements. The guidelines for both writing and evaluation have been written with the assumption that a congregation has identified its key elements.

Once a congregation has the six key elements clearly in mind, they can use the information either to evaluate published curriculum resources or to begin the process of creating their own resources. Congregations can follow the directions given in parts 2, 3, or 4 depending on their goals.

Each congregation will want to identify one person, such as the pastor, educator, or chair of the Christian education committee, to oversee the curriculum evaluating or writing process from beginning to end. Congregations that are without a trained staff person can appoint a team of two or three people. The shared responsibility of this team is to oversee the continuity of the evaluation or writing process.

Commitment, time, and energy are required on the part of educational leaders whether using the guidelines in this book for evaluating curriculum resources that already exist or for creating your own. The end result, however, will make all the effort worthwhile. The hard work will enable you to have a curriculum that is "just right" for your congregation's educational ministry. While a "perfect" curriculum may not exist, it is possible to find, create, or adapt a curriculum that will nurture the faith of your congregation's members, call them into a relationship with Jesus Christ, support your congregation's educational goals, and be an effective tool for your educational ministry.

PART 1

Identifying a Congregational Purpose for Christian Education

Assessing Your Christian Education Program

Your congregation members are unhappy with the curriculum resources you are using. The teachers complain that there are not enough activities for the kids to do and that the lessons are hard to prepare. The kids say the lessons are boring, and they vote by not coming back to Sunday school. The parents complain that they don't know what is happening at church school because their kids don't bring home take-home papers or artwork. The older people complain that kids aren't memorizing Bible verses the way they did when they were young. Perhaps you have heard all these complaints and many more.

When you go to a Bible bookstore or denominational resource center, you will find a huge variety of curriculum materials from which to choose. Some resources are bright and colorful; some have craft kits you can buy; some have CDs with fun songs; some say they are easy for teachers to prepare; some have newsletters for parents. How do you choose the right one? Which one will satisfy the needs of your congregation? Which one lines up doctrinally with your tradition? You may begin to think you would be best off writing your own!

If you have ever been responsible for choosing and/or providing curricula for the Christian education programs of your church, this is probably an all too familiar scenario. Faced with so many choices, it is hard to know what criteria to use. You may select the denominational resource or the one that looks easiest for teachers to prepare or the one with the brightest cover. You may discover that there really isn't a single resource that offers everything for which you are looking. You may leave the store or resource center completely confused by the overwhelming nature of the choices.

Many congregational committees charged with planning an educational ministry are deciding to write their own curriculum. By writing their own, they can at least get the qualities they want in one resource. They can choose the

Bible passages to teach, design the program for the class sizes they actually have, make the lessons easy for their teachers to prepare, and use a nontraditional model, such as workshop rotation, if they want.

Unfortunately, too much value has been placed on the curriculum resource itself. Churches hope that the right materials—either purchased or written in-house—will solve all the problems facing Sunday schools—and churches—today. They wonder if the right print materials will make it easier to recruit teachers who will stay for the whole year, excite kids so they will want to come to church school every Sunday, teach the Bible so children and youth will know its stories and teachings, and attract young families so they will join the church and support its ministry.

One of the most frequently cited reasons for choosing a certain curriculum series is that teachers want a quick preparation time. In our busy lives, those who volunteer to teach on Sunday mornings want materials they can prepare in a short time. A frequent incentive for agreeing to teach in the first place is that it won't take a lot of time. Nevertheless, the required preparation time should never be the primary reason to choose a prepared resource.

Many teachers—both those currently teaching and those being recruited—may feel unqualified to teach. They question their own biblical knowledge and understanding. But unfortunately, in the busyness of life, time for training and equipping teachers is harder and harder to find. So many congregations are resorting to handing a curriculum to teachers and hoping they will show up when they are expected.

One consequence of this minimalist course of action is the absence of goals for educational ministry. When education committees do not take time to determine the purpose of their education program, the program lacks the organization needed to connect curriculum, teacher training, and evaluation with ministry goals. Without clear direction, more and more emphasis is put on finding the "right" curriculum.

Thus, great expectations are placed on the materials used in educational ministries. And frankly, there is no curriculum resource—already written or to be written by you—that will single-handedly turn around declining membership or lack of congregational commitment in any church. Still, it is possible to select or write a resource that will enrich the educational ministry of your church, strengthen the faith of those who participate, support your teachers, and turn a mood of discouragement into a sense of direction and purpose. Such a transformation depends on first understanding the appropriate role of curricula in the overall educational ministry of your church. It requires recognizing that no single resource can do everything.

The Latin root of the word *curriculum, currere,* means "to run the race." Think of the way the word is used in other settings. A high school or college curriculum refers to all the courses a student will take to move the student toward the goal of graduation. If churches will redefine their use of the word *curriculum* to mean the whole task of calling people to faith and nurturing their discipleship, then the curriculum resources become one of the elements of the entire "curriculum" and curriculum returns to its appropriate role. Although it is not within the scope of this book to address the other components beyond print and media resources that compose a church's education "curriculum," I do encourage you to develop plans for training, supporting, and recognizing teachers, and for evaluating the educational program and introducing new resources.

The first step in moving from frustration over a disorganized educational ministry to hope is to identify clearly the purpose and goals of Christian education in your church. Without such an understanding of where you want to go and what you want to accomplish, it is impossible to choose or write a resource to help you fulfill those goals and purposes.

Once your purpose and goals have been articulated and claimed, choosing curriculum resources to buy becomes much easier and the process of writing your own resources receives clarity and direction. The prepared resources you use will then move you toward your goal, your Christian education program will be strengthened, and you will be able to focus on the other elements of "running the race."

Now when you make a trip to the bookstore or resource center, you will have a clear sense of purpose and will be able to evaluate resources based on whether they will support your educational ministry. The characteristics will be clear, the criteria will be easy to measure, and your decisions can be made with purpose. You will know the questions to ask and the characteristics for which to look. You will leave the bookstore filled with excitement and a sense of faithfulness to the ministry of your church.

Educational Purpose

The process of identifying the purpose and goals of your educational ministry begins with some basic questions:

- What is a Christian?
- How do people become Christians?
- How do people grow as Christians?
- What is the Bible?
- How do we use the Bible to support growth of Christian faith?
- What is the mission of the church?
- What is the role of the church in nurturing the growth of a Christian's faith?
- How does the church teach Christians?

Discovering the answers to these questions has everything to do with the curriculum you use. Without an understanding of what a Christian is, how a person becomes a Christian, and how a person grows in his or her faith, it is impossible to make any decisions about a print or media resource to support the growth of that faith. Without an understanding of the role of the Bible in nurturing Christian faith, you can have no direction for what to teach. Without an understanding of how you want to transmit faith from one person to another and from one generation to another, your plan for educational ministry will have no integrity or consistency.

The process of selecting curriculum resources that are right for your church begins with understanding your congregation. Each congregation has its own traditions, perspectives, programs, and activities. Each congregation has a certain way of understanding their ministry. Choosing or writing curriculum begins with knowing the personality of your congregation—its perception of the mission of the church and its preferences for communicating Christian faith.

Many congregations would probably say that making disciples is the goal of their educational ministry. However, a wide diversity of opinions exists about what it means to be a follower of Jesus Christ. Reaching a consensus about the meaning of Christian faith is the first step in any curriculum choice. For that reason a congregation needs to examine what they believe about God. These are theological questions.

Likewise, there are many ways to understand the use of Scripture and its role in our faith lives. Without a clear statement about Scripture, it is impossible to establish how the Bible will be studied. Does it contain history or story or science or moral instruction? Is it the job of the believer to interpret or memorize Scripture or study it as literature? A congregation needs to explore their beliefs about the Bible and the way to interpret and use Scripture. These are biblical questions.

Furthermore, the educational process has to be matched to the purpose and goals the congregation has set. If you live in Kansas City and want to reach Hong Kong, a car is not a mode of transportation that will enable you to reach your goal. Rather, you need to choose a means of transportation that is appropriate to your goal. The same is true in Christian education: methods and practices need to be appropriate ways to reach your goals. Therefore, congregations need to discuss how faith is passed on to determine the best education methods and practices.

All these questions and others beg for answers long before a congregation can make a decision about resources for their educational ministry. The collection of information about your congregation may seem overwhelming at first, but the process described in this handbook will break down the information into several well-defined, easy-to-use steps.

2 Centrality of the Six Key Elements

Six key elements form the foundation of this workbook. Each one defines and describes a particular component of educational ministry. They are the necessary building blocks for evaluating and writing curriculum resources.

Key 1 is a statement of the purpose or goal for Christian education in your church. It will answer the question about what a Christian is and how disciples are formed through education. This may be the most difficult part of the workshop process and the one element about which you have the most discussion. However, once the purpose of your educational ministry is named, the remainder of the elements will be easier to identify.

Key 2 concerns your congregation's understanding of the Bible and how it should be used in the educational programs of your church. Discovering a wide variety of views of Scripture within a congregation is not unusual, so asking questions regarding the biblical understanding of your denomination or tradition will be helpful at this point. The statement of biblical use should reflect that tradition as well as the opinions of those on the Christian education committee. When in doubt it is best to lean toward the beliefs of your tradition.

Key 3 provides an overview and summary of all of the settings for educational ministry in your congregation. This includes Sunday school, youth group, adult classes, women's or men's groups, and the like. Along with the list of settings, you will include curriculum resources currently in current use and numbers of participants. The curriculum used with children and youth on Sunday morning is most often the primary subject of discussion and dissatisfaction.

Key 4 addresses the content to be taught in your educational programs. While it may be simple to answer that the Bible is of course the content of education in the church, different views of Scripture result in different visions of content. For instance, the Bible may be viewed as a moral guidebook, a collection of stories, or a historical platform from which to reflect on contemporary issues. As you plan your curriculum resources, you will need to identify the content in more concrete terms than simply "the Bible."

Key 5 defines the role of teachers/leaders in your educational ministry. Is the teacher the expert and authority figure who tells the students what they need to know? Or is the leader a facilitator who invites learners into the study of the Scripture? The language you use can reflect the congregation's perception of those who teach and those who learn.

Key 6 defines the role of students/learners in your educational ministry. Is the task of the student to repeat back what the teacher has said, or does the learner engage with the content in a variety of ways under the direction of a leader?

Together the responses for Keys 4 and 5 compose your educational theory. They describe in practical terms how disciples will be taught and formed. These two keys together will determine the way the content is developed and the kind of activities that will be included in the curriculum.

Getting Organized for the Workshops

The workshop process described here will involve a group of people in your congregation concerned with Christian education who will meet in two sessions, one for an hour and the other for ninety minutes. At the end of these two sessions, this group of people will have determined the six key elements for your church. The workshops involve a variety of participatory activities than enable members to discern their theological, biblical, and educational perspectives and to discuss them with others.

In light of busy schedules, engaging in concentrated study of educational ministry is often difficult for congregations. The workshop designs that follow recognize this challenge and offer ideas for streamlining the work to honor the value of people's time.

As you invite participants, tell them why their time will be well spent. Your enthusiasm for the task can encourage others to come with energy and excitement. Help participants understand the exact amount of time the two workshops will take and what is expected from them. Share with them that the outcome of their time and effort will be a clear direction for the Christian education programs of your church.

The people you invite to be part of this committee should represent groups within the congregation who are involved in educational ministry already, such as youth, parents of church school students, Christian education committee members, and others. Try to find people from both genders in a variety of ages. Six to twelve members make a good size for a working group.

Explain to participants that it is important that they plan to attend both meetings and to arrive on time. Assure them that every effort will be made to begin and end on time. It is possible to do both workshops on one day—such as a Saturday. However, be aware that back-to-back sessions eliminate the chance to reflect in between and to gather needed information.

As you prepare to lead the committee through the two workshops, be sure that you have read through the design, gathered all the supplies, copied the handouts, and set up the meeting space as suggested. If you are ready when the group arrives, you can keep your promise to limit the time of the meeting.

Once the six key elements are apparent, you will be ready to evaluate purchased curriculum or to organize to develop your own. Part 2 of this workbook will show you the importance of these elements in evaluating printed curriculum. Part 3 will enable you to use the key elements to organize and write your own curriculum resources.

Exploring Our Ministry

Goal: To identify Key 1—the purpose of educational ministry

Expected Outcomes

- Participants will reflect on the goal of Christian education in their congregation.

- Participants will determine the position along the continuum that best represents their congregation.

- Participants will write Key 1 based on their discussion and insights.

Time: 1 hour

Materials: masking tape; copies of Worksheets 1 and 2; newsprint and markers, or overhead projector, transparencies, and pens, or computer with PowerPoint and projector

Room Setup: In an open area of the meeting space, place a twenty-foot strip of masking tape along the floor. Set up a table and enough chairs for the group.

Preparation: Before the group gathers, set up a way to record where the participants stand along the continuum. You can use newsprint, an overhead transparency, or PowerPoint to reproduce the continuum. During the activity be sure you or someone else records the position of the group members along the continuum so everyone will be able to see the results when the activity is complete.

Opening (10 minutes)

Welcome everyone and have group members introduce themselves. As an ice-breaker, ask each person to say one thing he or she likes about the current educational program of the church.

Open with prayer.

Explain that the overall goal for this workshop and the next one is to identify key elements of the church's educational program that will be used as a foundation statement for decisions the church will be making about curricula. Give the participants a copy of Worksheet 1 or point out the newsprint, overhead, or PowerPoint with the list of the six key elements. Read through the elements and explain that the goal of this first workshop is to identify Key 1—the purpose of educational ministry within your congregation. Also explain that the success of the process depends on everyone participating and sharing his or her ideas.

Use the Continuum (10 minutes)

Point out the masking tape you have placed on the floor. Explain that you will read a series of statements (from Worksheet 2) and they are to position themselves along the masking tape to indicate where on a continuum they belong. If they agree mostly with the A statement, they are to move toward the left end of the masking tape; if they agree mostly with the B statement, they are to move toward the right end. If they think both statements are true to a degree, they are to move toward the center of the tape.

Read the sets of statements one at a time and give the group members time to arrange themselves along the tape. Remember to record the response of each person to each set of questions on a reproduction of the continuum that you made prior to the group meeting.

Discuss the Results (10 minutes)

When you have read all of the statements, have the group members sit down again. Use the reproduction of the continuum so that participants can see results. Give them a copy of Worksheet 2 so they can see the questions. Invite them to discuss the results of the activity. Ask these questions: What surprises you most about the results? What do you think it says about this church? What does it tell you about the perceived goal of Christian education in this church?

Write Key 1 for Your Congregation (30 minutes)

Look at the responses to sets of questions 1–4 about the mission and ministry of the church. Encourage the group to identify the characteristics of the mission and ministry of the church about which they agree. Write these phrases on newsprint, overhead, or PowerPoint. Remember that there may be a variety of opinions. The goal of this activity is to find the things the whole group can agree on.

Next, look at the results of questions 5–7 about the purpose of Christian education. Repeat the activity of identifying and recording the things about which the group can agree.

Invite the group to discuss any trends they are seeing. Ask the following questions: What is emerging out of this process? Where is the agreement? Where are the differences? In what way are these results consistent with your experiences in this church?

Ask the group if they are ready to write Key 1—the purpose statement for their educational ministry. Refer to the words and phrases the group agreed on that you have recorded from the statements on the mission and ministry of the church and the purpose of Christian education. Encourage group members to discuss the connections between purposes for Christian education and the mission and ministry of the church. Use newsprint, overhead, or Power-Point to write out their suggestions for Key 1.

Have the group write Key 1 on their copies of Worksheet 1: Six Key Elements.

Explain that questions 8–10 will be used in determining Key 2 when the group meets the next time. Confirm the time and place for that workshop.

Close the meeting with prayer.

Six Key Elements

Key 1: Purpose or goal for Christian education in your church

Key 2: What the Bible is and how you use it in your educational ministry

Key 3: Settings for educational ministry in your congregation

Key 4: Content to be taught in your educational ministry

Key 5: Role of teachers in your educational ministry

Key 6: Role of learners in your educational ministry

Educational Ministry Continuum

Before each pair of statements, instruct participants that if they agree mostly with A, they should move toward the left, and if they agree mostly with B, they should move toward the right.

1. Which of the following statements do you think best describes the mission and ministry of the church?

   A. The mission of the church is to save souls.

   B. The mission of the church is to redeem society.

2. Which of the following statements do you think best describes the mission and ministry of the church?

   A. The mission and ministry of the church is to call individuals to a personal faith in Jesus Christ.

   B. The mission and ministry of the church is to invite individuals into the community of faith in which they worship, learn, and serve.

3. Which of the following statements do you think best describes the mission and ministry of the church?

   A. The purpose of the church is to provide a guide for moral conduct and Christian living.

   B. The ministry of the church is to guide people with a biblical understanding of God's purpose in the world as they seek to transform the world.

4. Which of the following statements do you think best describes the mission and ministry of the church?

   A. The ministry of the church is to teach God's Word, teach people how to please God through obedience, and teach people to move closer to Jesus.

   B. The purpose of the church is to nurture the community of faith and to encourage members to reach out into the life of the world.

5. Which one of the following statements do you think best describes the purpose of Christian education?

   A. The purpose of Christian education is to teach people about Jesus Christ and to lead them to accept him as their personal Savior.

   B. The purpose of Christian education is to provide an opportunity for people to respond to God in faith, love, commitment, and obedience.

6. Which one of the following statements do you think best describes the purpose of Christian education?

   A. The purpose of Christian education is to help people learn Bible truths that can aid them in daily living.

   B. The purpose of Christian education is to enable people to interpret the biblical message and its meaning for today.

7. Which one of the following do you think best describes the purpose of Christian education?

   A. The purpose of Christian education is to teach people Christian codes of conduct and instruct them in the morally right way to live.

   B. The purpose of Christian education is to enable people to understand their denominational heritage and to participate in the community of faith.

8. Which of the following statements do you think best describes the Bible and its use?

   A. The Bible is literal and without error.

   B. The Bible tells of the work of God in the words of human beings and reflects the culture of those who wrote it.

9. Which of the following statements do you think best describes the Bible and its use?

   A. Bible study is the only appropriate subject for Christian education.

   B. Any subject can be studied from a biblical perspective.

10. Which of the following statements do you think best describes the Bible and its use?

    A. Bible study should teach moral and behavioral concepts.

    B. Bible study should allow learners the opportunity to interpret the Scripture.

WORKSHOP 2
Examining Our Ministry

Goal: To identify Keys 4–6

Expected Outcomes

- Participants will determine their preference for teaching, learning, and content to be taught.

- Participants will write Keys 3–5.

- Participants will learn about the students and the classes of the current Christian education program.

Time: 90 minutes

Materials: copies of Worksheets 3 and 4; pens or pencils; copies of Worksheet 1 with Key 1 added; newsprint and markers, or overhead projector, transparencies, and pens, or computer with PowerPoint and projector

Room Setup: chairs around a table

Preparation: Prior to the workshop, make a reproduction or master list of Worksheets 1 and 4 on newsprint, overhead transparency, or PowerPoint. Whichever format you use, be sure that you can mark the participants' votes beside each item. Complete Worksheet 3: Christian Education Information with the data you have collected about your educational programs.

Opening (10 minutes)

Welcome the group members and open with prayer.

Explain that during this workshop the group will be identifying Keys 4–6. Tell them that you will present the information you gathered for Key 3 so that at the end of the workshop all six key elements will be complete.

Give the group members copies of the revised Worksheet 1 and ask them to read through Key 1, which they wrote during the previous workshop. Invite them to suggest any adjustments to it that they think will strengthen it.

Find Out about the Present Educational Program (10 minutes)

Give group members a copy of Worksheet 3 with the information you have collected about the current programs of your educational ministry. Explain that this handout identifies Key 3. Answer any questions they may have about the programs.

Identify Priorities (45 minutes)

Have the group members look at the results of questions 8–10 about the Bible on Worksheet 2, which they completed during the first workshop. Repeat the activity of identifying and recording you used in the first workshop to identify the things about the Bible on which the group can agree. Invite the group to discuss any trends they are seeing. Ask the following questions: What is emerging out of this process? Where is the agreement? Where are the differences? In what way are these results consistent with your experiences in this church? Use their responses to compose Key 2.

Give the group members copies of Worksheet 4. Point out that there are sets of four statements in each letter group. Explain that they are to work individually and choose the one statement in each group that they think is the truest or most important. Give the group members about 5 minutes to make their choices.

Next, call the attention of the group members to the reproduction you have made of the statements. Explain that the group votes will be recorded on the reproduction. Read each set of statements one at a time and have each group member share how he or she voted. On the master list, use hash marks to record the votes of group members next to each statement. When the group has read through all the sets of statements, total the number of votes for each statement and cross out the statements that receive no marks.

Invite the group members to examine the master list. Ask the following questions: What trends do you see? What agreement do you see between the statements in the different sets? What is most surprising to you? Do you agree or disagree with the trends? Do you think the trends are reflective of the educational ministry of this church? Why or why not?

Write Keys 4, 5, and 6 (15 minutes)

Use the reproduction of Worksheet 1: Six Key Elements and fill in the statements that the group members choose as the top priorities.

Under Key 4 write the statements from sections A–E about content that received the most votes. Under Key 5 write the statements from sections F–H about teachers who received the most votes. Encourage the group members to write the responses on their own list of key elements as you go along. Under Key 6 write the statements from sections I–L about learners that received the most votes. Have the group look through what you wrote.

Divide learners into three small groups and ask each group to write one of the key elements. Give each group newsprint and markers. After about 15 minutes, gather the whole group back together. One at a time invite the small groups to read what they have written. After each small group reports, encourage the rest of the group to respond and to make adjustments to the wording.

When the wording for each of the key elements meets the approval of the whole group, write them on your master copy of Worksheet 1: Six Key Elements.

Tell What Comes Next (10 minutes)

Tell the group that they have now completed all six keys. Invite them to talk about the process and the results. Ask the following questions: What do you think of the six key elements you identified? Do you think they reflect the church as a whole? What do you like/dislike about this whole process now that we are done?

Remind the group that these six key elements will be used next either to evaluate published curriculum resources or to form the foundation of materials the church will write. Ask whether any of them would be interested—and willing—to serve on the next committee to make decisions about curricula.

Thank everyone for participating.

Close by singing the Doxology or a worship chorus together.

Christian Education Information

Name of Church _____

Address _____

Phone _____ E-mail _____

Classes Now in Session

Fill in the following information about classes presently meeting.

	Age	Curriculum	Number on Roll	Number Attending
1.				
2.				
3.				
4.				
5.				
6.				
7.				
8.				
9.				
10.				
11.				
12.				

Questions for Sorting

In sections A–E choose the two topics that you think are most important to be taught in educational programs. Give your top priority two marks and the second priority one mark.

A. ____ Focus on Bible stories
____ Meaning of biblical truths for today
____ Chronological overview of Old and New Testament
____ Study of major biblical themes such as covenant, redemption, and law

B. ____ Nature and mission of the church
____ Christian discipleship
____ Nature and revelation of God
____ Issues related to family 1ife

C. ____ History of the church
____ Understanding of Jesus Christ as personal Savior
____ Responsibilities of church membership
____ Diversity of God's people

D. ____ Understanding and development of personal uniqueness and potential
____ Personal character and morals of Christians
____ Major theological concepts of our denomination
____ Techniques and resources for critical biblical study

E. ____ Studies of missions
____ Worship history and traditions
____ Contemporary issues and problems
____ Political responsibility

From each group of statements in sections F–L, choose the one you think is important or true and mark your response.

F.   ____ Teaching is enabling persons to do their own learning.
  ____ Teaching is relating to other persons with trust, love, and acceptance.
  ____ Teaching is attempting to convert others to the teacher's ideas and beliefs.
  ____ Teaching is helping persons see alternatives and make responsible choices.

G.   ____ Teaching is providing an example to follow.
  ____ Teaching is witness to what one believes.
  ____ Men make better teachers of adults while women make better children's teachers.
  ____ Teaching calls for advance preparation.

H.   ____ Teaching is presenting the lesson.
  ____ Teaching is planning a session or meeting so that the group is interested.
  ____ Teaching is imparting knowledge.
  ____ Teaching is asking the students to receive, memorize, and repeat.

I.   ____ Persons learn in terms of what is significant to them.
  ____ Learning has taken place when new information has been given.
  ____ Learning involves the whole person, not just the mind.
  ____ Learning leads to a change in behavior, attitudes, skills, and knowledge.

J.   ____ Learning is a lifelong process.
  ____ Learning takes place primarily during childhood.
  ____ Learning takes place in all church activities, not just in planned education activities.
  ____ Learning is relating new information to past and/or present experience.

K.   ____ Adult learn differently than do children and youth.
  ____ Learning can be increased if group is mixed in age, sex, race, etc.
  ____ Learning requires grouping persons of similar age and interest.
  ____ The condition of the room influences learning.

L.   ____ Learning is increased by student participation through such things as discussion and doing research.
  ____ Each person must do his or her own learning, though others may help.
  ____ Learning is highly influenced by everyone in the group, not just the teacher.
  ____ Learning is almost completely dependent upon the teacher.

Evaluating and Choosing Curriculum Resources

3 Acknowledging Christian Education Assumptions

Part 2 of this handbook will enable you to use the six key elements that you identified in the Part 1 workshops to evaluate and choose published curriculum materials for your congregation. The value of your efforts during the workshops will be evident as you learn to use the key elements to examine resources.

As noted earlier, congregations often make decisions about printed resources on the basis of appearance and cost. They want materials that are colorful, that have extras such as craft kits and student books, and that are affordable. During the evaluation process suggested here, you will need to refrain from using such criteria as your standards and choose a curriculum resource by drawing on your congregation's six key elements.

Curriculum resources created and sold by publishing companies, both denominational and independent, are all written from certain theological and biblical perspectives. They engage an educational approach that they believe supports those particular perspectives. Since one size does not fit all, it is important to know the biblical tradition and educational approach of your congregation and of the curriculum. The knowledge of both will contribute to the selection of a curriculum resource that will enable you to meet your congregation's goals for its educational ministry.

Workshop Assumptions

An important first step in preparing to evaluate published curricula is to identify the theological and educational assumptions and perspectives held by the publisher. Only when you have identified the assumptions within the curriculum will you be able to compare them with the six key elements you have determined reflect the educational ministry of your congregation.

It is one thing to say that a congregation should match the biblical, theological, and educational perspectives of a published curriculum to their congregation's six key elements but quite another to actually do it. This can be a daunting task! Certain words and phrases frequently used by publishing houses in association with certain theological and educational assumptions can make your task easier. You can use these words and phrases as clues to the perspective and goals of a printed curriculum.

In the following section, each assumption is defined and then followed by a series of statements representing two ends of a theological and educational continuum. These are the same sets of statements used in Worksheet 2, so refer back to it if you like. Each set of statements is followed by words and phrases frequently used in printed resources to describe the curriculum.

First, identify the statements that most closely agree with your congregation's. As you examine curriculum materials, you can watch for these words and phrases. Although the system is not perfect, it does offer a way to eliminate many of the resources that do not match your six key elements and are inappropriate for your congregation.

Publishing House Assumptions

Assumption 1: The first assumption concerns the publishing house's understanding of what a Christian is and how Christian faith is nurtured. Another way of expressing the same thing is to talk about the mission of the church. The goal of the curriculum is to support that particular understanding. The purpose of the curriculum needs to support the goal of your educational ministry as stated in Key 1.

This aspect of a published resource is the most important for you to evaluate. The purpose of a curriculum should be clearly stated in the beginning of a resource. Once you have found it, you can compare that statement with your congregation's Key 1. If they are not in harmony with one another, you will know that you can put that curriculum aside and not consider it further—regardless of how attractive or inexpensive it may be.

If you believe that

- the mission of the church is to save souls and to call people to a personal faith in Jesus Christ
- the purpose of the church is to provide a guide for moral conduct and Christian lives

then you will want to look for the following words and phrases in published resources:

- Lead people to salvation in Christ; lead people from sin to life in Christ

- Teach perspectives of God's plan for salvation

- Teach the attributes of Jesus and how to follow his model

On the other hand, if you believe that

- the mission of the church is to invite individuals into the community of faith in which they worship, learn, and serve

- the purpose of the church is to nurture the community of faith and to encourage members to be guided by a biblical understanding of God's purpose as they reach out into the life of the world

then you will want to look for the following words and phrases in published resources:

- Explore relationship with God and community

- Encourage active participation in worship and service of the church

- Promote service to others

Assumption 2: The second assumption concerns the publishing house's understanding of Scripture and its role in the life of a Christian. If the resource is at odds with your tradition's understanding of Scripture, then again the curriculum will not assist you in reaching your goal for ministry. During Workshop 2 you identified your congregation's view of Scripture in Key 2.

Another helpful clue in identifying a view of Scripture is to determine the version of the Bible recommended and used in the material. If it is not the version most frequently used within the educational settings and worship of your congregation, you will probably discover other incompatibilities in biblical assumptions.

If you believe that

- the Bible is literal and without error

- Bible study should teach concepts

then you will want to look for the following words and phrases in printed resources:

- Bible truths and values

- Know Bible facts

- Application of biblical values to daily life

If you believe that

- The Bible tells about the work of God in the words of human beings and reflects the culture of those who wrote it
- Bible study should invite learners to interpret the Scripture

then you will want to look for the following words and phrases in printed resources:

- Develop skills for interpretation, including critical biblical scholarship
- Explore the overall story of the Bible
- Connect the story with experience of learner

Assumption 3: The third assumption addresses age groups and settings in the church for which the curriculum is written. For instance, there are materials for elementary school children to be used during a church school and there are materials developed for youth groups in a Sunday evening setting. As you evaluate curriculum resources, you will need to examine materials that are appropriate for the age group and for the setting you need. In Key 3 you identified all the learning settings in your congregation and the printed resources being used.

Don't overlook including the purchased resources you are currently using in your evaluation process. The current curriculum can be tested against these assumptions and evaluated using your six key elements. You may find that these materials are a good match.

Assumption 4: A fourth assumption concerns the publishing house's choice for the content of its printed curriculum or the way it chooses to organize the content. It is important that you decide on the content you want to teach rather than having it first determined by the curriculum. For instance, if your goal is to teach the great stories of the Bible to younger children, then a curriculum that uses only small portions of Scripture and a focus on Bible truths will not match your goal of having children learn Bible stories.

To identify the content of a curriculum, look for a chart providing the Scriptures, themes, and/or key ideas. Such a chart is usually found in the front of the leader's guide. A review of this chart will enable you to compare the scope of the content and organization of it with the content you want to teach. Again, it is important to ask whether the content will help you to reach the overall goal of your educational ministry.

If the purpose of your educational ministry is to lead each student to Jesus Christ as Savior and to know his will and obey him, then you will look for curriculum content such as the following:

- Meaning of biblical truths for today
- Understanding of Jesus Christ as personal Savior

- Personal character and morals of Christians

- Application of biblical truth to all of life

- Development of personal faith of learner

- Evaluation of life in light of biblical message

If the purpose of your educational ministry is to invite individuals into the community of faith in which they worship, learn, and reach out into the life of the world, then you will look for curriculum content such as the following:

- Biblical stories

- Overview of Old and New Testament

- History of the church

- Contemporary issues and problems, including political responsibility

- Diversity of God's people

- Major theological concepts of your faith tradition

- Techniques and resources for critical biblical study

Assumption 5: Also embedded in each published curriculum are certain understandings about how people learn their faith. These assumptions become explicit in the teaching methods used. They include an understanding of the roles of both teacher and learner. In Keys 5 and 6 you have identified your congregation's understandings of how teaching should be done and how people learn their faith. These educational concepts should match the educational theory of the purchased resources.

The best way to evaluate teaching methods and understanding of how people learn their faith is to read through several session plans. Notice what kind of role the teacher or leader plays in these sessions. Is the teacher given a script? Are correct answers provided to questions? What kind of activities are used to engage the learners? Are the activities much the same, or is there a lot of variety? How are the students involved in the learning process?

Read the objectives or purpose of each session and think about how these stated purposes will enable your learners to reach your congregation's educational goals.

If you believe that

- teaching needs to provide people with guidance that can help them in daily living

- teaching gives people Christian codes of conduct and instructs them in the morally right way to live

then you will want to look for the following words and phrases in printed resources:

- Teach fundamental knowledge of God

- Change hearts of children and behavior of children

- Show ways to put values into practice

If you believe that

- teaching provides an opportunity for people to know God and respond to God in faith, love, and commitment

- teaching enables people to understand the biblical message and its meaning for today

then you will want to look for the following words and phrases in printed resources:

- Develop skills for reasoning things out for themselves

- Equip learners to struggle with complex moral issues

- Encourage learners to do their own learning

Using the Assumptions

The words and phrases associated with the two ends of the theological continuum have been grouped together on Worksheets 5 and 6 so you can make easy use of the assumptions about the mission of the church, the Bible and the purpose of educational ministry. On Worksheet 5—"Key Words and Phrases—Salvation"—you will find the key words to look for if you believe that the purpose of educational ministry is to bring people to salvation in Jesus Christ. On Worksheet 6—"Key Words and Phrases—Community"—you will find the key words to look for if you believe that the purpose of educational ministry is to building a community within which people worship, learn, and reach out into the life of the world.

As you examine curriculum to be included in the curriculum evaluation process, the worksheet will help you find the best matches for you congregation. This will enable you to eliminate from consideration, curriculum resources that are not appropriate for your congregation and will not serve as tool for reaching your educational goals.

By matching the publisher assumptions with the six key elements you have identified for your congregation you will be able to find a curriculum that enriches your educational ministry. Such a match will strengthen the total ministry and will enable you to reach the goals you have set.

Key Words and Phrases—Salvation

The purpose of our educational ministry is to lead each student to Jesus Christ as Savior and to know his will and obey him.

Look for contents of curriculum, such as:

- Meaning of biblical truths for today

- Understanding of Jesus Christ as personal Savior

- Personal character and morals of Christians

- Application of biblical truth to all of life

- Development of personal faith of learner

- Evaluation of life in light of biblical message

We believe that the mission of the church is to save souls and to call people to a personal faith in Jesus Christ.

Look for the following words and phrases in the curriculum:

- Lead people to salvation in Christ, to lead them from sin to life in Christ

- Teach perspectives of God's plan for salvation

- Teach the attributes of Jesus and how to follow his model

We believe that the Bible is literal and without error and that Bible study should teach concepts.

Look for the following words and phrases in the curriculum:

- Bible truths and values

- Know Bible facts

- Application of biblical values to daily life

We believe that teaching gives people Christian codes of conduct and instructs them in the morally right way to live.

Look for the following words and phrases in the curriculum:

- Teach fundamental knowledge of God

- Change hearts of children and behavior of children

- Show ways to put values into practice

Key Words and Phrases–Community

The purpose of our educational ministry is to invite individuals into the community of faith in which they worship, learn, and reach out into the life of the world.

Look for contents of curriculum, such as:

- Biblical stories

- Overview of Old and New Testament

- History of the church

- Contemporary issues and problems, including political responsibility

- Diversity of God's people

- Major theological concepts of your faith tradition

- Techniques and resources for critical biblical study

We believe that the mission of the church is to nurture the community of faith and to encourage members to be guided by a biblical understanding of God's purposes as they reach out into the life of the world.

Look for the following words and phrases in the curriculum:

- Explore relationship with God and community

- Encourage active participation in worship and service of the church

- Promote service to others

We believe that the Bible tells of the work of God in the words of human beings and reflects the culture of those who wrote it and that Bible study should invite learners to interpret the Scripture.

Look for the following words and phrases in the curriculum:

- Develop skills for interpretation, including critical biblical scholarship

- Explore overall story of the Bible

- Connect the story with experience of learner

We believe that teaching provides an opportunity for people to know God and respond to God in faith, love, and commitment.

Look for the following words and phrases in the curriculum:

- Develop skills for reasoning things out for themselves

- Equip learners to struggle with complex moral issues

- Encourage learners to do their own learning.

4 Initiating the Evaluation Process

Once you have identified the six key elements of your congregation and have a basic understanding of the assumptions made by publishing houses, you are ready to evaluate curricula and to make a choice for your church. In preparation for a workshop to evaluate curricula, you will need to do three things:

1. Invite a group of people to participate in the evaluation process.

2. Gather four to eight curriculum samples to evaluate that represent the perspectives and goals of your educational ministry.

3. Do a cost assessment of the curriculum samples the group of volunteers will evaluate.

The process will move more smoothly—and quickly—if the same committee that identified the six key elements for your congregation also makes the final decisions about a published curriculum to be used at your church. They will already be thoroughly familiar with the key elements and therefore will be competent in using them in the evaluation process. The evaluation workshop will take about an hour and a half. However, if the group members are already familiar with the six key elements and were involved in creating them, the evaluation process may be finished even more quickly.

If it is necessary to invite people not involved in the previous process, be sure that they have the opportunity to study the six key elements before Workshop 3: Curriculum Evaluation. You may want to ask them to read through Worksheets 2 through 4 ahead of time so they will have thought through the questions and become familiar with the concepts behind each of the key elements. Introducing the key elements to a new group of people will of necessity make the workshop longer. Be sure that new people understand that the evaluation workshop is not a time to rewrite the key elements.

Ways to Acquire Curriculum Samples

Publishing companies and denominational offices are more than glad to send you promotional materials about their curricula. However, it is necessary to have actual curriculum samples at the workshop so that committee members can view the product. They should be able to read through a lesson plan, examine the student books, and see the teaching aids.

There are several sources for curriculum samples. If you have a resource center in your area, you may be able to borrow samples. Sometimes denominational offices have samples available of curricula endorsed or sold by the denomination. You may be able to borrow samples of curricula being used by other churches in your area. Your church may have received sample packets or advertisements about curriculum resources. Check with your pastor, church secretary, or church school teachers. And go to the websites of curriculum publishers. They will be glad to send you samples, but be sure to allow time for shipping.

A way for you as the educator or committee chair to expedite the evaluation process is to select for review by the committee only those curricula that are consistent with your church's biblical perspective, educational goals, and needs. As you make choices about which samples to provide for the committee to evaluate, watch for key words and phrases that are consistent with those you have already identified as the church's perspectives in the six key elements. You can use Worksheets 5 and 6 to aid you in the process.

The kind of samples that you obtain will depend on the setting and age groups of the students. If you want to find a curriculum that you can use in the Sunday school for ages zero to ninety-nine, then you will provide several series for the workshop. If you are looking for materials to use for a short-term study for a narrow age range on a specific topic such as baptism or confirmation, you will obtain several stand-alone resources.

More often than not, congregations take the time to evaluate curricula when they are seeking material to use in the whole church school. As you prepare for the workshop, you and the education committee will need to decide whether you want to be able to mix and match curricula—in other words, whether the children use one series, the youth another, and adults still another series. You need to be ready to explain your expectations to the evaluators.

Cost Assessment

Prior to the workshop, you will need to do a cost assessment for each curriculum series you will present to the committee to evaluate. At the end of this chapter you will find Worksheet 7: Curriculum Cost Assessment. Prepare one for each of the curriculum that you have chosen.

For each curriculum series that you are considering, include the detailed information about costs for the number of teacher's books, student books, and classroom resources you will need. For example:

Name of Curriculum: **Growing in Faith**

Publisher: **Our Curriculum**

Age Group: **Kindergarten**

Cost for Teacher's Book: **$4:00**	Number of Teacher's Books Needed: **3**	Total: **$12.00**
Cost of Classroom Activity Packs: **$10.00**	Number of Packs Needed: **1**	Total: **$10.00**
Cost of Student Books **$1.00**	Number of Students: **10**	Total: **$10.00**
Cost of Other Resources: **0**	Number Needed: **0**	Total: 0

Age Group: **Elementary**

Cost for Teacher's Book: **$6.00**	Number of Teacher's Books Needed: **2**	Total: **$12.00**
Cost of Classroom Activity Packs: **$10.00**	Number of Packs Needed: **1**	Total: **$10.00**
Cost of Student Books: **$1.00**	Number of Students: **10**	Total: **$10.00**
Cost of Other Resources: **24.00**	Number Needed: **1**	Total: **$24.00**

Total for Curriculum: **$88.00**

You will need this information for the evaluators during the workshop when they are ready to make a final selection. In order to do this you can use the Curriculum Cost Assessment Worksheet on the next page. Make a copy for each curriculum. Have copies of this information available at the workshop. While the decision about curriculum should not be made based on price, it certainly can be a factor. Knowing the prices of curriculum may enable the committee to choose between their top two final choices.

Curriculum Cost Assessment

Name of Curriculum

Publisher

Age Group

Cost for Teacher's Book	Number of Teacher's Books Needed	Total
Cost of Classroom Activity Packs	Number of Packs Needed	Total
Cost of Student Books	Number of Students	Total
Cost of Other Resources	Number Needed	Total

Total for Curriculum

Age Group

Cost for Teacher's Book	Number of Teacher's Books Needed	Total
Cost of Classroom Activity Packs	Number of Packs Needed	Total
Cost of Student Books	Number of Students	Total
Cost of Other Resources	Number Needed	Total

Total for Curriculum

Age Group

Cost for Teacher's Book	Number of Teacher's Books Needed	Total
Cost of Classroom Activity Packs	Number of Packs Needed	Total
Cost of Student Books	Number of Students	Total
Cost of Other Resources	Number Needed	Total

Total for Curriculum

WORKSHOP 3
Curriculum Evaluation

Goal: To select a printed curriculum resource

Expected Outcomes

- Participants will become familiar with or review the six key elements of the congregation.

- Participants will evaluate several published curriculum resources.

- Participants will review ways in which publishing house assumptions are consistent with the congregation's six key elements.

- Participants will choose among the curriculum resources.

Time: 60–75 minutes

Materials: several print curriculum samples, Worksheet 7: Curriculum Cost Assessment for each curriculum sample, copies of the congregation's six key elements, copies of Worksheet 8: Curriculum Evaluation, copies of either Worksheet 5 or 6 (based on your congregation's goal for educational ministry), pencils, newsprint and markers, index cards.

Room Setup: Set up a table in the center of the room with chairs for everyone on the committee. You will need a small table for each curriculum sample to be reviewed. Along with the sample, place on each table copies of Worksheet 8: Curriculum Evaluation, pencils, a piece of newsprint, and markers. Place the small tables around the outside of the room or in another room.

Preparation: Collect four to eight samples of published curriculum and complete a cost assessment for each curriculum.

Opening (5 minutes)

Welcome the participants and open with prayer.

Explain that during the session the group will be examining several curriculum resources and by the end of the session will be ready to choose one for use.

Introduce the Six Key Elements and Assumptions (10 minutes)

Give each participant a copy of the six key elements. If this document is new to these people, introduce them to the key elements and tell them briefly about the process of identifying them. If this is the same group of people, review the six key elements they have identified in the earlier workshops. Explain that the group will be using these six key elements to evaluate sample curricula to determine whether they are consistent with the church's goal for its educational ministry.

Based on your congregation's goal for educational ministry, give members of the group copies of either Worksheet 5 or 6. Explain that each publishing house also has assumptions about the goal of educational ministry, use of Scripture, and educational methods. Tell them that the handouts represent publishing house assumptions that are closest to the congregation's goals and perspective. Tell them that as they review curriculum, they can be looking for words and phrases that match the goals and assumptions of their congregation.

Evaluate Curriculum (20–30 minutes)

Point out the curricula on the tables around the room. Based on the decisions of the Christian education committee, tell the group they will be evaluating a series for use within the whole educational program or looking for the best curricula to be used by different age groups for a special study. If you are searching for a series, be sure the evaluators understand whether they can mix and match resources for age groups.

Explain that each person will evaluate two or three of the samples. Ask at least two individuals to examine each curriculum. Depending on the number of curriculum samples and the number of teams, you may want to assign certain curricula to certain individuals to assure that all the samples will be examined.

Point out the copies of Worksheet 8: Curriculum Evaluation on each table. Tell the group members that each evaluator will complete one of the forms for each of the curricula he or she evaluates. Ask them to give each curriculum an overall rating for consistency with the purpose of the congregation's educational ministry. Give the committee members about 20 to 30 minutes to examine the curricula.

Choose a Curriculum Product (30 minutes)

Gather everyone back together. As a group walk around the tables holding the curriculum samples. One by one ask those who reviewed the curriculum to share their evaluations. On a piece of newsprint, create a master list. Record the name of each curriculum and all the numerical ratings it received from the evaluators. As the group moves around to hear the evaluation for each curriculum, add the name and ratings to the newsprint. At the end of the time, you will have a list of the curriculum and the scores each received. Add the combined ratings for each sample and divide by the number of reviewers to find its average rating.

Identify the two or three resources that ranked highest and take them to the center table. Pass out the cost assessments you completed earlier for these curricula. Discuss the costs of the curriculum plus the strengths and weaknesses of each curriculum.

Ask the group whether they are ready to make the decision about which of these resources will best strengthen and enable your educational ministry. If you already have consensus, then the decision is made. If a decision is not clear, take a vote. Pass out index cards and ask group members to vote for their first choice. Based on this vote, make a final choice about the curriculum that will best enhance your educational ministry.

Give thanks to everyone and close with prayer.

Curriculum Evaluation

Name of curriculum:

Publisher:

Denomination (if identified):

Age groups:

Setting (Sunday school, youth group, midweek program, etc.):

Purpose of curriculum:

View of Scripture:

Recommended or quoted version of the Bible:

Role of teacher:

Role of learner:

On a scale of 1 to 5 (with 1 being the lowest) rate this curriculum in its consistency with the purpose of the educational ministry in your congregation:

1   2   3   4   5

PART 3

Writing Curriculum Resources

5 Get Ready

The decision to write your own curriculum resource is a big one and not to be done without careful thought. Many times congregations make the decision to write their own material out of frustration with available curriculum rather than out of a desire to provide quality resources. But the decision to write your own materials requires commitment to a complex, long-term process and should be made only after careful consideration.

Churches often choose to write their own educational resources for one of three main reasons. One of those reasons is that they have not been able to find a published curriculum that matches their particular perspectives or is culturally appropriate. A curriculum may be too difficult to teach, may not provide the same understanding of Scripture as the congregation, or may lack the desired extras, such as take-home papers and teacher aids.

As cited in part 2 on curriculum evaluation, all resources come with their own perspectives. Each publishing house has its own assumptions about goals of educational ministry, roles of learners and leaders, and use of Scripture. By using the process outlined in part 2, congregations can identify these assumptions and compare them with their own assumptions outlined in their own six key elements. That is an important first step if you are considering writing your own resources.

A second reason congregations choose to write their own curriculum is because they have selected a particular model for their educational ministry, such as workshop rotation. In that case they may not be able to find prepared resources that are consistent with the interest areas or Bible stories they have chosen.

Finally, a church may choose to write curriculum because they have not been able to find resources for a particular study emphasis they want to include for children, youth, or adults, such as preparation for baptism or confirmation or for study of a church season. By writing their own materials, they can include the topics and perspectives that match the needs of their particular congregation.

The purpose of part 3 is to give you detailed guidance for the process of writing educational materials for your congregation. If you are thinking about writing your own resources for the first time, I encourage you to read all of part 3 before making a final decision. If you are already writing resources and want suggestions for improving the process, please also read through all three chapters of part 3. You will learn how to prepare your own curriculum by applying the six key elements to each step of the writing process. This is the best way to assure that the outcomes reflect your congregation's understanding of what a Christian is and how Christians are formed and educated.

While writing your own curriculum is both time and energy consuming, it can also bring a great deal of satisfaction. It involves the pleasure of seeing teachers ready and eager to teach and learners excited about learning. Those who write curricula often find that their own faith is enriched and deepened through the process of developing resources for others to use. Having materials that enable you to reach the congregation's educational goals makes the time and energy spent well worth the effort.

Determine Who Makes Decisions

Each congregation will organize to write their own curriculum materials in the way that works for them and takes advantage of the gifts available within the congregation. Generally, however, there are some decisions that those charged with the oversight of the educational ministry will need to make and other decisions that the writing team will make. It is important to distinguish the responsibilities of each group.

Those who give oversight to the whole Christian education program will want to make the initial decision to develop curriculum resources for their congregation. Because they are familiar with all the goals and components of the program, they are the people who should determine what is best for the congregation's educational ministry. They have reviewed the entire program, established a purpose and direction for the ministry, and identified the congregation's understanding of Scripture and the educational process. They are positioned to use the six key elements to get the stage ready for the writers.

Those charged with oversight of the educational ministry are the ones who will decide the setting and age groups for which curriculum resources will be written and the content to be taught. In some cases they will also be the ones to establish the scope and sequence of the curriculum. If the preparation of curricula for all ages in the church school is under consideration, the educational ministry committee will determine both the content and sequence. In the case of a short-term study, the educational ministry committee will determine the themes, age group, and setting while the writing team sets up the details of the content and the order in which it will be taught.

The size and composition of the writing team will vary from congregation to congregation, depending on the scope of the material and variety of settings for the intended resources. At the very least, two people should write so that the final product does not represent only one person's perspective. On the other hand, a writing team should be limited to five or six people, for it can be cumbersome for a larger group to write together. Another option would be to have several teams, each of which would write for a different age group.

In some churches writers develop the themes, select the biblical passages, and develop the outlines. They also develop the session plans. Other congregations have one group that determines the themes, Scripture portions, and outlines, and another group that does the actual session writing.

There are a lot of ways to organize the writing of resources and to involve people in the process. But regardless of how many people do the writing and how the tasks are distributed, it is essential to have one or two people assigned to provide project oversight and editing. These people will be responsible for being sure the writing is done on time and for reading the materials for consistency with your six key elements. They may also make final adjustments to the language and/or grammar.

As you consider the people within your congregation who could serve as part of the curriculum writing team, keep in mind the following qualities:

- Willingness to commit the necessary time for writing and meeting with the team

- Familiarity with the basics of English grammar

- Ability to write clear instructions for others to use

- Experience as a church school teacher

- Commitment to educational ministry

- Dependability

- Creativity

- Familiarity with the variety of ways in which people learn

Determine Educational Settings

The first step in the process of writing your own printed resources is to determine the educational settings in which you are currently using printed resources and where new resources are needed. Begin by reviewing the information you compiled for Key 3. At that point you completed a list of educational settings in your church and the curriculum used in each setting. Begin by asking for which setting you have been unable to find resources that match your educational ministry goals, the age group, and your congregation's understanding of Scripture. Where is the greatest need? It for this setting that you will want to begin to develop your own curriculum.

You may decide that the Sunday church school is the setting where your own curriculum resources are most needed. Begin by deciding whether you will develop resources for all age groups or concentrate on a single group, such as elementary age children, middle high youth, or adults.

Since writing curriculum is both time and energy consuming, I recommend that you start small rather than beginning with resources for your whole educational program. Start with a very narrow focus in terms of age group, theme, and setting. This will give you a chance to try out writing your own resources as well as developing a system to support the creation of your own curriculum. By starting small you will have the opportunity to gauge the time and energy involved, identify people with writing and editing skills within the congregation, and discover your design and production options.

Writing curriculum is a huge undertaking, and it may not be right for your congregation. Certainly it is better to discover that with a small project rather than after deciding to develop curricula for all elementary age classes for a whole year. You may discover that it takes more time and energy than you imagined or that willing writers are not available or that there are too many things to manage.

If you are already writing your own curriculum and hope to learn some new approaches from this book, your learning may be facilitated by applying the principles I present in the following pages to a short study. You will thus be able to compare your current practices with the suggestions I offer.

The following sections are intended to direct you, enable you, and inspire you as you write your own resources. Each step of the process will be outlined and described in detail with specific examples. Copy Worksheet 9: Curriculum Overview, and as you complete each of the steps, fill in the results of your decision making.

Determine the Content

Once you have determined the setting and age group for which you will develop resources, you will be ready to consider the content that you will teach. The information you gathered during the earlier planning workshops will be especially valuable. For this step in the writing process, you will want to look at Keys 2 and 4.

In Workshop 2 you considered your church's beliefs about Scripture along a continuum. You decided whether you most closely believe that the Bible is literal and without error or that the Bible tells of the work of God in the words of human beings and reflects the culture of those who wrote it. Your position along this continuum will affect the way you use the Bible in the curriculum resources you write.

You were also asked to decide whether Bible study is the only appropriate subject for Christian education or whether any subject can be studied from a biblical perspective. Your answer to this question will affect the use you make of Scripture. It will determine whether your resources will involve only studies of the Bible or whether you will engage in studies of a wide variety of subjects.

Finally, you were asked whether a Bible study should teach moral concepts or allow learners the opportunity to interpret the Scripture. Your response to this question will determine the learning goals you set for students. In addition, the responses will influence the objectives you set and the teaching methods you choose.

If for some reason you did not use the workshops to identify your congregation's position along these continuums, you need to do so now. Without an understanding of your church's understanding of how to study Scripture and use the Bible, the curriculum you write will not enable you to reach your educational ministry goals.

During the earlier workshops, you were asked to rank a variety of topics for educational studies. Either review your previous choices or consider the topics below. By each letter of the following list, mark your first and second choices. Your choices will guide as you select the content for your writing.

A. Biblical truths for today, chronological overview of the Bible, or biblical themes

B. Mission of the church, nature and revelation of God, or issues related to family life

C. History of the church, understanding of Jesus Christ as personal Savior, or diversity issues

D. Character and morals of Christians, denominational theology, or critical biblical study

E. Missions, worship history and traditions, or environmental responsibility

Mission Study Sample

As a way of illustrating the particulars of each step, a six-part study of missions for fourth and fifth graders will be used as a sample. This study is intended to replace the regular church school curriculum for six weeks. Throughout the rest of this chapter, this mission study will be used as an example for each step in the process. You will be able to compare the specifics of the example with the specifics you create for your own studies.

The following information is used in this example:

Setting: church school

Age group: fourth and fifth graders

Content: missions

Determine the Scope and Sequence

Once you have determined the setting, age group, and content, you are ready to move on to the next step. Now you will use both the congregation's understanding of the use of Scripture and the priorities you set for content to develop a scope and sequence for your curriculum resources. In this part of the process, you will begin to give shape to the general goals of your ministry and move toward the specific content of your resources.

Scope

Regardless of what kind of study you choose to write, you will begin with the subject or content. The scope defines what aspects of the content you will cover in the curriculum. It narrows down a wide topic such as the Bible or salvation into manageable units that give focus to the topic. It describes the material you want to include. The scope provides the parameters for the content of your teaching.

For instance, you may want elementary children in the Sunday school to study the whole Bible in a six-year period. So the Bible is the wider scope. But since that is much too wide to be manageable, at this point you will want to identify a scope for each year within the six-year cycle, perhaps spending three years on the Old Testament and three years on the New Testament. The next step is to identify the scope for each year.

Year 1: Genesis to Joshua

Year 2: Samuel to Chronicles

Year 3: Prophets

Year 4: Gospels

Year 5: Paul's Epistles

Year 6: General Epistles and Revelation

The content of the sample study is missions. But that is much too wide to be manageable, so you need to narrow the scope. The scope for the mission study could include the following:

• Biblical passages from Luke and Acts about missions

• History of missions in your denomination

- Contemporary missionary activities of your denomination
- Suggestions for ways in which learners can be involved in missions

Before going any further in the preparation of your study, determine the scope for your curriculum. What do you want to focus on and include? If you decide to do a short-term study or special session for one age group, the scope will be narrow. If you decide to write material for the entire elementary church school for a whole year, the scope will be much broader. Either way you will need to determine an exact description of the scope of the study. Record the scope on Worksheet 9: Curriculum Overview.

Sequence

Once you have determined your scope, you will need to decide the sequence or organization of the content. There are a variety of ways to do this. You can organize stories by the order in which they occur in Scripture, that is, chronologically. Or for a biblical theme such as covenant, salvation, or revelation, you can order the stories or passages chronologically or thematically. If you want to emphasize certain behaviors or life applications, you can organize units around particular behaviors or values.

In the example of a yearlong study of Genesis to Joshua, you could do the following:

- Organize the stories chronologically.
- Select biblical characters to use as models for a specific behavior.
- Identify a biblical concept such as covenant and study its development.

In the example of a mission study for fourth and fifth graders, there are at least two ways to organize the sequence. One way would be to use a portion of Scriptures as the basis of each session. Each session would include accounts from the history of missions or contemporary missionary activities as well as an activity for the learners. A second way to organize the sequence would be chronologically, beginning with Jesus and moving through mission history up to the current time. This sequence could also include an activity for the learners.

Themes and Scriptures

Next you will make the sequence even more specific by creating a title/theme with accompanying portions of Scripture for each session. You can begin by deciding first on either the thematic title or the biblical passage. Look through the sequence of your sessions and decide which method will work best for your purposes.

Perhaps the selection of the biblical passages is already clear. If you are doing a chronological study of Genesis to Joshua and want the learners to hear the two stories of Creation, then the passages from the first and second chapters of Genesis are obvious. However, if you are doing a study of major characters in the first six books of the Bible and want to explore the story of Joseph, you will have to decide which verses in chapters 37 through 50 of Genesis you will use. Your choices will depend in part on the age of the learners and the number of sessions you will spend on the Joseph saga.

If you begin with the biblical passage, the title/theme will provide an overview or indication of what the session is about. Titles can be descriptive or suggestive. For example, the story of Joseph and his brothers in Genesis 37:2-4, 12-35 could be titled "Joseph and His Brothers," "A Coat of Many Colors," or "A Pit, a Sale, and a Lie."

Or you can begin with a behavior, such as courage, and choose different aspects of courage on which you want to focus. For example, one session could consider courage in the face of physical danger and another session on the courage required to stand up to unpopular opinions. Many biblical passages could be used for each of these examples of courage. Brainstorm possible portions of Scripture and then choose among them for the best Bible selection to go with the theme.

In the ongoing sample of the mission study, the sequence will use scriptural passages to organize the study. Each session will include a passage from Luke or Acts and will examine the commands of Jesus and the actions of the new church. Each session will also include a story of a historical or contemporary missionary as well as suggestions for ways learners can engage in mission activities.

Setting: church school

Age group: fourth and fifth graders

Content: missions

Scope: missionary stories from Luke and Acts, historical and contemporary stories, activity suggestions for learners

Sequence: Jesus > coming of Holy Spirit > events in the early church

Session themes and Scriptures:

    Week 1: Jesus Sends Out the Seventy (Luke 10:1-12)

    Week 2: Jesus Commissions His Followers (Luke 24:36-53)

    Week 3: The Holy Spirit Comes (Acts 2:1-13)

    Week 4: Peter and John Heal a Man (Acts 3:1-10)

    Week 5: The Baptism of the Ethiopian (Acts 8:26-40)

    Week 6: The Call of Saul (Acts 9:1-19)

Curriculum Overview

Setting:

Age group:

Content:

Scope:

Sequence:

Session themes and Scriptures:

6 Get Set

In chapter 5 you identified the educational settings and age groups for which you want to write curriculum materials. You also decided on the subject matter for your curriculum and developed a scope and sequence for the sessions.

In this chapter you will learn how to move from the scope and sequence you identified for the sessions within your study to an outline that writers can use to develop the content for each session plan. First, you will learn how to explore each biblical selection and to utilize the results of the exploration in building the sessions. Next you will learn how to write a main idea, goal, and outcomes for each session for the writers to use as outlines. Finally, you will develop a session structure that will be used to direct the flow of each session. Your fleshing out these components for each session will give the writers a strong foundation for developing themes and concepts. You will find that the time and energy you expend in exploring Scripture, identifying the main idea, goal, and objective, and planning a common structure for each session is well spent.

Exploring the Biblical Passage

Once you have identified the scope and sequence, as well as the themes and biblical passages for your curriculum, you are ready to explore the biblical content. The results of this exploration will be used to write the main idea for each session, to define the goal and expected outcomes, and to equip the writers and teachers with background information about the passage. Regardless of your understanding of Scripture and whether you are planning a Bible study or another kind of study based on a biblical perspective, it is essential that you engage in exploration of the biblical content in preparation for writing.

One person on the writing team can be appointed to do all the biblical exploration, or it can be divided up among the writers. Perhaps there is someone in the congregation not on the writing team, such as the pastor, who has training in biblical studies who would agree to do the Scripture study for your curriculum. Whoever does the study can use Worksheet 10: Biblical Exploration for each passage to make the information available to the writers and teachers.

It is not possible to overemphasize the importance of engaging in an exploration of the scriptural passages you will use for your curriculum. Sometimes we are tempted to impose a meaning on a passage, making it say what *we* want it to say. Biblical exploration offers us the opportunity to discover what *God* has to say and protects us from the human tendency to make Scripture say what we want. If after doing biblical exploration you find that one or more of the passages you have chosen do not actually support the theme, you can do further exploration to choose replacement passages.

Following is a five-part framework for exploring biblical passages. There is room on Worksheet 10: Biblical Exploration to record the information for each passage you have chosen. Make copies of the worksheet for each biblical passage or enter it into your computer to record the results electronically. Once the biblical exploration for all the passages is completed, make copies for each member of the writing team.

Step 1: Study the Passage.

Begin by reading the passage in several translations of the Bible. Parallel versions of the Bible that include more than one translation are available in print and online and give you the ability to compare translations side by side. As you read, notice words and phrases that seem important. Make a note of any words or names that you do not know or that seem confusing. List any questions you have about words, people, or places in Step 4 on the worksheet. Note that words may vary from translation to translation. Pay attention to what seems important to you about the differences.

Now go back and read the passages that come immediately before and after the section you are studying. Ask what was happening and what was said. Consider how the material previous to your passage is related to what happens or is said in your passage. Think about how the actions, events, and dialogue that follow relate to the passage you are studying. On the worksheet, write a short paragraph stating the main ideas or concepts of the passage. Finally, review any other Scripture that is referenced or quoted within your passage. Often the Old Testament is referred to within the New Testament books.

Step 2: Study the Words about God.

Think about what the passage has to say about God. In the outline, write several words that describe God or God's actions in the passage. Is God loving or judgmental? Does God work behind the scenes, or is God active? Does God speak to anyone? What does God say?

Ask yourself what the passage says about humans and the connection between God and humans. Write down a few descriptive words about humans. What are the humans doing? What kind of human behavior is rewarded or judged? What do you think God wants the human creatures to do? Are they obedient or sinful? Do they act in response to God or in spite of God?

Finally, ask yourself what kind of response the person reading the passage is called to make. What new or changed behavior does this passage encourage or suggest? Write down one or two ideas in the outline.

Step 3: Study the Background of the Book.

Each book of the Bible was written within a historical period and for a particular purpose. Understanding the original context and purpose can enrich the study of each passage. You can look up this background information in a Bible dictionary, study Bible, or one-volume commentary. Find out when the book was written, who wrote it, and why it was written. Include this information on your worksheet.

Step 4: Study Important Words.

As part of step 1, you wrote down your questions about words, people, or places in this section of the worksheet. Now look up these words, people, or places in a Bible dictionary and write in the information you find. Writers will use this information when they develop background sections for the teachers.

Step 5: Study the Concepts.

As a last step, you are ready to hear what other people think about the passage. Read one or more commentaries about the passage. Write down any new ideas you discover. Now compare the thoughts of others with what you wrote in Step 1. Revise or adapt what you wrote based on the ideas you found in commentaries. Write a final main idea in two or three sentences.

Once you have completed the biblical exploration, there are three ways you can use your information. (1) You can use it to develop the main idea for each session. (2) You can use it to give direction to the writers so that the activities they include are a reflection of the biblical study. (3) You can use it to enrich the teaching of the leaders as they introduce the Scripture to learners. It will give them a glimpse into the biblical setting and introduce them to the theological themes.

Spending time as a writing team discussing the passages will also be helpful. The person who did the biblical exploration can introduce what he or she found out about the passage, and other team members can reflect on the passage and share their own insights. This will greatly enrich the writing process as well as deepen the understanding of each writer.

A variety of Bible study resources are listed at the end of this chapter. Visit your denominational bookstore or online booksellers for additional suggestions. You may want to check your church's library and your pastor's library as well.

Determining the Main Idea, Goal, and Outcomes for Each Session

Once the biblical exploration is complete, you are ready to create outlines to be used by the writers in developing each session. Make a copy of Worksheet 11: Session Outline for each session you are planning. Transfer the themes and the biblical passages for the sessions from Worksheet 9: Curriculum Overview to each session outline. You can also do this part of the process electronically by putting Worksheet 11: Session Outline on your computer.

During this final step of "Get Set," you will confirm the main idea, decide on a goal and outcomes for each session, and add those to the session outlines. When these outlines are complete, the writers can begin their work of fleshing out the main idea and session goal with guidance for the teachers and activities for the learners to do.

Main Idea

A main idea states the major ideas and concepts of a passage. The person who did the biblical exploration took main ideas from the passages as part of the exploration process. Read through the main idea and consider the ages of the learners. Ask whether the concepts in the main idea are appropriate for them. You may determine to limit the concepts for younger learners and expand them for older students.

Copy the main idea into the session outline. The main idea will be included at the beginning of each session plan. Writers will use these statements to maintain a consistency between their activities and the main idea. Teachers will use the main ideas to evaluate the sessions. For example, the main idea for the whole mission study for fourth and fifth graders could read, "Jesus calls his disciples to go out into the world and to tell everyone about him and his love. Over the centuries many people have answered that call. Today we can still answer Jesus' call to go and tell others."

Goal and Outcomes

A goal narrows the focus of all the things there are to know or understand about God or the Bible. A goal can be understood as a step toward the wider purpose of educational ministry. Goals are written from the perspective of the teacher.

They provide the focus for the session and describe the hope, vision, intention, and direction of the session. A goal does not, however, describe specifics about how it will be reached. In fact, a goal, as I'm using the term here, cannot be reached. An example of a goal for the mission study is "To learn about missions." There is no way to learn all there is to know about missions from this one study. It would take a lifetime to do that.

Outcomes, however, are attainable, specific, and measurable. They describe in concrete terms exactly what the learner will know or be able to do at the end of the session. Teachers should be able to look at the written objectives after a session is completed and know whether the learners reached these outcomes. For instance, an outcome may be: "Learners will become familiar with the names and stories of three prophets." The writer's task is to develop sessions in which the students will learn about three prophets. And the teacher of these sessions should be able to confirm that the students did indeed learn the names and stories of three prophets.

Theme: Peter and John Heal a Man

Bible passage: Acts 3:1-10

Main idea:
In the days following Pentecost, Peter and John were on the way to the temple to worship when they stopped to heal a man in the name of Jesus. As some of the first missionaries, Peter and John model for us the idea of sharing whatever we have with others. The man who was healed shows us the importance of responding with joy to God's good gifts.

Goal:
To hear the story of Peter and John and to think about gifts learners have to share the good news with others.

Outcomes:
- Learners will be able to retell the story of Peter, John, and the lame man.
- Learners will think about the gifts they have for sharing God's love with others.
- Learners will identify a way they can share the good news with someone.
- Learners will celebrate God's love.

Determining the Structure for an Individual Session

The final step in getting ready for writing is to set up an individual session structure or outline that will be used throughout the curriculum. Using the same structure for the sessions will contribute to the ease of both writing and teaching. The structure provides a guide for the movement or flow of the session from introduction of the main idea to the conclusion of the lesson time.

The structure will help the writers by enabling them to ask such things as how to begin, how to connect with learners, how to close the session, and so on. Rather than being a hindrance to creativity, the structure will enable writers and teachers to move in a consistent manner through each session.

Each session needs to have an opening, a way to present the main idea, a way to develop that idea and invite the learners to respond, and a way to close. You can rename each section of the structure with a name of your own choice or just use the descriptive phrases given in the Session Outline worksheet. Regardless of what you call them, each session will need the following parts:

Opening. The opening provides a way to welcome learners into the learning space and into a time of learning. Writers will want to include suggestions for ways to set up the room, ways leaders can engage learners as they arrive, and ways to set the stage for the person or subject to be discussed. This is a time to set the tone for the session.

Presenting the main idea. The presentation of the main idea, whether it is a Bible story, a theological concept, or a moral value begins after the opening when everyone has arrived. Depending on the age group, the writers have a wide variety of choices about how to present the idea or concept. Above all, the idea or concept needs to be presented clearly so that the learners can understand it and respond as the lesson proceeds.

Exploring the main idea. This aspect of the session provides ways for the learners to explore, interpret, and preserve the main idea. This is also the part of the session in which they will consider the ways in which the main idea relates or applies to their own lives. A variety of activities in this section of the lesson will keep learners interested and involved.

Responding to the main idea. This section of the structure invites the learners to make a response to the main idea, concept, or story. This is the way they engage with the concept or idea, relate it to their own experiences and lives, and make a response of some kind, showing their learning. Just as there are a wide variety of ways to present a main idea, there are many ways to invite learners to respond.

Closing. The closing pulls all the other parts of the session together. It is a time for summary of the main idea and celebration of what has been learned and a time to say good-bye to the learners.

Biblical Exploration

Step 1: Study the passage.

Step 2: Study the words about God.

Step 3: Study the background of the book.

Step 4: Study important words.

Step 5: Study the concepts.

Sample Biblical Exploration Worksheet

Scripture: Acts 3:1-10

Step 1: Study the Passage.

Acts 1 opens with Jesus' ascension into heaven and his charge to the disciples to be his witnesses in the world. Christ then commands them to wait for the coming of the Spirit. Acts 2 gives the account of Pentecost, at which time the disciples were baptized with the Holy Spirit. Peter speaks to the crowd, proclaiming that Jesus of Nazareth is the long-awaited Messiah. The third and fourth chapters focus on the healing of the lame man. When pressed by the authorities, Peter point outs that it was not his or John's own power or piety that gave healing to the man but rather their faith in the name of Jesus.

Main Idea: Peter and John encounter a lame man on their way to pray in the temple. The man asks the disciples for money, which they do not have, but they give him what they *do* have. Speaking in the name of Jesus, they heal the man. He responds by leaping and praising God. The story reminds us that we each have gifts to offer and that the proper response to God's grace is praise and thanksgiving.

Step 2: Study the Words about God.

Jesus as God's Son is able to change lives and offer new life. God is able to do things that seem impossible to humans. In the healing of the man through Peter and John, Jesus offered the man a new way to live.

Peter and John had no money to share, but they trusted Jesus. When they spoke Jesus' name they believed that God would be faithful to their request and heal the man. They acted and showed a belief in the reality and power of the resurrected Christ.

The lame man responded in the only way he could. He stood up, felt the strength in his legs, and began jumping and leaping around the courtyard. He gave thanks, and the other people who saw him wanted to know what had happened.

Peter used the opportunity to talk about Jesus—both his identity as Son of God and his power to do amazing things. Peter called those who listened to believe and become followers of the Christ.

Step 3: Study the Background of the Book.

The book of Acts tells the story of the church's origin, early mission work, and growth from Jerusalem to Rome and the ends of the earth. The same Luke who wrote the Gospel of that name also wrote Acts. The two books are linked together by their common address to Theophilus. Scholars believe the book was written around A.D. 60.

The book of Acts seeks to tell the story of the spread of the good news of Jesus Christ from its beginning at Pentecost in Jerusalem to a worldwide movement. It follows the story of the church as it moved from Jerusalem to Judea to Samaria to Antioch to Ethiopia to Asia Minor to Macedonia and eventually to Rome. Notable in the book are the accounts of Paul's missionary journeys during which he told the good news to Gentiles—people who were not Jews.

Step 4: Study Important Words.

Three o'clock in the afternoon. This was the time of afternoon sacrifice and a common time to go to the temple for prayers and worship.

Beautiful Gate. One of the entrances into the Jewish temple in Jerusalem. It was common for beggars to sit by the gate and ask for money from those going into the temple. Some scholars question this designation and think it is a reference to the Nicanor Gate, a gate made of bronze.

Jesus' name. The Jews, from biblical times through today, believe that there is tremendous power contained in the divine name. To speak God's name is believed to endow the speaker with the power of that name. The name of God represented the divine power behind it. That belief has been carried into Christianity and applied to our belief in the power of Jesus' name.

Step 5: Study the Concepts.

This passage invites us to think about more than money when we reflect on what we have to give. The disciples had their faith in Christ to share as well as God's gift of healing.

The story reminds us that social or economic standing has nothing to do with what we have to give. Everyone has something to share. Peter and John offered healing in the name of Jesus; the lame man offered God his exuberant joy. His enthusiastic response to God's graciousness moved others to repent and believe.

The passage reminds us that everything we offer in the name of Christ is a good gift and that God can use what we offer to spread the good news of Jesus.

Session Outline

Theme:

Bible passage:

Main idea:

Goal:

Outcomes:

Supplies:

Opening:

Presenting the main idea:

Exploring the main idea:

Responding to the main idea:

Closing:

7 Go

Now you are ready to pass the biblical exploration and the session outlines into the hands of the writers. Before you do that, however, you will need to provide some training for your writers—both an introduction to the work already done by the education committee and some specific how-to directions for the writing. It is important that writers have both an overview of the six key elements and a familiarity with the practical ways the key elements will impact their writing.

You need to plan time to bring the writers on board and to make your intentions for their writing clear and exact. Time spent training the writers will give the materials they produce uniformity and consistency with the goals of your educational ministry. In the long run this will increase the ease with which teachers will be able to use the materials.

You may want to plan a training retreat for writers and go away so that you can give complete attention to the writing process. Or you may want to use a workshop format and hold one or two events to prepare writers. Whatever format you decide to use, offer the writers an opportunity to learn about the work the educational committee has done in identifying the six key elements. They should become familiar with the scope and sequence as well as the intent behind the choices of themes and biblical passages. A writers' retreat provides time for you to give explicit directions for their writing and for teams to get acquainted. Training events build the bridge for the writers between the theory of the six key elements and their writing. It is vital that writers understand—and agree with—the larger purpose of educational ministry in your congregation as stated in Key 1. This purpose gives direction for the materials they will write.

One outcome of training the writers is to equip them with the skills for translating that purpose into the teaching plans they create. For instance, if the goal for your educational ministry is to provide a guide for moral conduct and for living Christian lives, then writers will need to understand how to strive toward that goal in each of the learning designs they develop.

A writer's retreat or workshop also provides the opportunity for writers to become familiar with the view of Scripture identified in Key 2, the broad scope of the content from Key 4, and the role of learners and teachers from Keys 5 and 6. You can explore with the writers an overview of the scope and sequence and themes and biblical passages for the sessions they will develop. A training event also allows you to demonstrate the style of writing you want writers to use and introduce types of questions, learning styles, and developmental characteristics.

Understanding the Roles of Teacher and Learner

Having a clear understanding of the roles of teachers and learners as expressed in Keys 5 and 6 is essential before the writers begin. Together these keys identify the educational theory in place within the congregation. Writers need to be able to use this theory in writing the session plans. The understanding of these roles is directly related to the goal of the educational ministry. Two methods—*transmission* and *inquiry*—represent two ends of a continuum describing the roles of teachers and learners.

Transmission Method

Congregations that understand that the goal of their educational programs is to call individuals to a personal faith in Jesus Christ, to provide a guide for moral conduct and Christian living, and to teach God's Word will prefer the transmission method. In this method the role of the teacher is to transmit information and facts to students. The students' role is to commit themselves to Jesus Christ and to change their behavior in accordance with what they are told about the lives of Christians.

The goal of the transmission method is for students to acquire knowledge and to learn facts and information. This method is considered to be "content centered." Frequently students are led or directed to a predetermined outcome. The role of the teacher is to tell students the facts and information and to lead them to accept correct doctrine, belief, moral rules, or behavior. The role of the student is to learn the information and to make changes in their behavior to conform with the moral rules being taught.

Sample goals for the transmission method may include the following:

- To help each other believe in Jesus

- To learn that the only way to obtain salvation is through Jesus Christ

- To learn that our obedience pleases God

Common objectives used with the transmission method include:

- Reading
- Repeating
- Discussing
- Practicing
- Remembering
- Applying

The whole movement of the session is focused on helping students to remember and repeat back the main point of the lesson or Bible truth. Discussions, games, and crafts all involve the repetition of that single concept. For instance, a game of tag may require that when the "tagger" tags someone, that person needs to say something he or she can do to help another person believe in Jesus. Crafts reinforce the lesson goal by having children add the main idea to some kind of paper format. For instance, the child may attach hands to a clock on which types of prayers have replaced the numbers.

The inclusion of scripts with the exact words to say for the teacher and answers to the questions are a regular feature of the transmission method. Your writers for this method need to be ready to create not only directions for teachers but also words for them to say and correct answers for questions.

Your choice about these features depends in part on your understanding of the roles of teachers and students. If having teachers say the information exactly is important to you, then including the words for them to say will enable them to do that. Some teachers consider this practice helpful, and others perceive it as limiting. One disadvantage to including a script is that a leader does not have to thoroughly understand the information only to read the printed words.

Inquiry

A congregation whose educational goal is to invite individuals into the community of faith where they worship, learn, and serve, to help people to be guided by a biblical understanding of God's purpose, and to encourage members to reach out into the life of the world will prefer the inquiry method. The role of the leader is to present information and facts and to facilitate the inquiry of the learners so they can interact with the information and deepen their own understanding of it.

In the inquiry method the goal is to bring together facts and information with experiences, feelings, and insights of learners. Often the method is referred to as "learner-centered" or "community centered" or "experiential." The role of the leader is to guide and direct the learners through a variety of activity-oriented techniques to interpret Scripture or find meaning in the themes. Learners respond to the topic or biblical passage by engaging in investigation, research, and reflection to reach their own conclusions.

Sample goals include the following:

- To deepen their understanding of the Holy Spirit
- To find ways to practice peace
- To learn about God's call and consider what God is calling them to do

Common outcomes or objectives include:

- Identifying
- Exploring
- Retelling
- Describing
- Researching

Because the goal of the inquiry method is to encourage and enable learners to engage with the Scripture or concept, activities are participatory and interactive. Crafts, such as making a desert collage from sand and different textures of paper, allow creative response. The use of music, rather than repetition of a concept to be learned, contributes to the understanding of the story. Learners might be asked to retell the story by writing a song to a familiar tune.

While the transmission method seems to focus on the salvation of each individual, the inquiry method often emphasizes the community aspect of the life of faith. Worship practice, seasons of the church year, lectionary, and the history of the church are topics included in curricula that value the communal life of God's people. Also frequently found in curriculum resources using the inquiry method is a concern for the needs of others. These resources often include a part in each session on ways learners can serve the church and community.

Within published curricula expressing a commitment to the inquiry method, it is becoming more and more common to find scripts for leaders and content answers for questions. I think this is perceived as being helpful to teachers. You will need to decide whether writers will use either of these practices for your inquiry method curriculum.

Writing for Others

Writing materials for others to use requires a different set of skills than developing a lesson plan for one's own use. When writing for others, the writer provides information and direction for someone else to follow without the benefit of the writer's presence. Therefore the writing needs to be clear and to the point.

A writer cannot assume that the teacher will know what is in his or her mind. Whereas lesson plans for one's own use can be brief and can contain shorthand directions, curriculum materials written for others need to include everything the leader needs to know to lead the activities, make the crafts, and give directions for games.

Curriculum materials are a like a conversation between a writer and the person who will use the materials to teach. They are a bridge between the thoughts and creativity of the writer and the actions of the teacher. The purpose of curriculum materials is to equip the leader to teach. If a teacher has to struggle over what to do or how to do it, the curriculum has failed the reach that goal.

Curriculum resources are written using the imperative voice—the voice used for giving orders, commands, and directions. A sentence in this voice begins with a directive word, such as *ask, tell, explain, invite, or show.*

Writers need to be constantly asking whether someone reading the directions will be able to do the activity based on their instructions alone. The writers will not be in the room with the teacher, so their directions must clearly describe their intent. When in doubt about the clarity of instructions, writers are encouraged to read the directions out loud to someone else to see if that person understands them. As a matter of fact, this is a good practice even if the directions seem clear to the writer.

Those who create curricula for publishing houses write to exact standards in terms of word count and page format. This is necessary so that manuscripts from writers will fill the space they have designated for a session and so that the lessons can be taught in the teaching time allowed.

Although you do not have the same restraints when creating your own curriculum, you may want to create guidelines for writers on the length of sessions. Teachers are not going to want to read activity instructions that take up three typed pages, but they are also not going to be happy if the directions are too brief. For your purposes it may work best to give writers a page count rather than have them worry about word count. For instance, you may set a limit of five to six typed pages for each session. Writers will then have the freedom to choose how many words they use for each section of the lesson.

Another thing to consider when giving directions to writers is the width of margins and line spacing. Those writing for publishers normally use one-inch margins and double spacing. Be sure your writers know how you want them to format the finished product they give to you.

Understanding Learners

In creating curriculum resources, writers need to have some knowledge about the many ways in which people learn and the different stages of human development. Familiarity with this information will enable writers to make their session activities and stories appropriate for a specific age group and sensitive to a variety of learning styles. An introduction to the Multiple Intelligences and age group characteristics can be found on reproducible handouts at the end of the chapter.

The Multiple Intelligences theory of Howard Gardner psychologist and professor of education at Harvard University's Graduate School of Education has received a lot of attention in the last few years among church educators. Gardner understands that intelligence is the ability to create problems to solve and then to solve them. Every person has preferred settings, experiences, and methods in which he or she likes to do that best. Gardner has named and described nine unique ways in which people prefer to express their ability to create and solve problems. You can find out more about Gardner's theory in his book *Frames of Mind: The Theory of Multiple Intelligences* (Basic Books, 1983).

Providing your writers with an introduction to learning styles will enable them to include a variety of activities in their learning plans. Recognition of the different ways people prefer to learn will lead to sessions that will appeal to a roomful of learners, all of whom enjoy learning in different ways. Writers can ask if they have included the following types of activities in each session: listening, doing, seeing, singing, moving, talking together, and reflecting individually. The more varied the activities within a single session, the more likely different kinds of learners will find that they can relate to some aspect of the lesson.

In the same way that lessons need to reflect a familiarity with differences in learning preferences, so sessions for different age groups need to consider their developmental characteristics. Human beings develop physically, emotionally, spiritually, and cognitively throughout their life span.

A way to express love and care for children and youth and to build their sense of worth as children of God is to create educational settings that are appropriate for their age groups. This includes the content of lesson plans as well as educational and behavioral expectations. For example, young children cannot yet think abstractly. They will only be able to talk about complex concepts such as love in terms of things they can see, hear, and touch. They will understand love best as it is expressed by the people who care for them.

The handout on developmental theory provides a brief introduction to the age group characteristics. For further information about each of these stages of development, consider purchasing a good reference book on age group characteristics, such as *Ages and Stages: A Parent's Guide to Normal Childhood Development* by Charles Schaefer and Theresa Foy DiGeronimo (John Wiley and Sons, 2000), or *Understanding Child Development* by Rosalind Charlesworth (Delmar Learning, 2004).

Public school teachers who are trained in developmental theory can provide additional information for writers. They may have books or manuals on human development that they can make available.

Asking Questions

The response a leader gets from learners to facts, information, or concepts depends in large part on the types of questions asked. It is vital that writers are familiar with the variety of choices they have for questions to include in resources. Each kind of question is intended to elicit a different kind of response from learners.

Content questions are based on facts and information. They demonstrate the student's ability to remember what has been taught. Following are some examples of content questions:

- Where was Jesus born?
- What were the names of Jesus' mother and father?
- What did the angel say to the shepherds?

While it is important to ask content questions, they are very limiting. Since learners can often respond with one or two words, this kind of question does not lead to discussion or conversation. If you want to encourage learners to discuss, express opinions, and interpret, encourage writers to avoid questions that can be answered with "yes" or "no."

In the transmission method the role of the teacher is to transfer information and a perspective to the learners. The role of the students is to be able to remember both the information and the perspective and repeat it back to the teacher. Content questions can be used successfully to determine what information or perspectives the students have remembered.

However, in inquiry, where the teacher's role is to present information inviting learners to reflect on that information and to explore it themselves, the use of content questions should be limited. Questions of this type will not encourage learners to interpret or analyze information for themselves.

Purchased curriculum resources using both the transmission and inquiry methods sometimes suggest right answers to questions. The answers are provided in parentheses after the questions. This can be a valuable practice for content questions but is less helpful if teachers want learners to relate the content to their own thinking and investigative processes. Your writers need to know whether to include answers to questions.

Analytical questions focus on concepts. Since there is more than one way to respond, these questions encourage learners to reflect on information and to form their own opinions and interpretations. The following are examples of analytical questions:

- Why do you think God sent Jesus to earth as a little baby?
- What do you think Mary thought about when she pondered all this in her heart?

- What do you think is the most important thing to remember about Christmas?

If your goal is to have learners repeat what the teacher has said, this kind of question is not helpful. If your goal is for learners to interpret and analyze the facts and information presented by the leaders, you will want to have writers include this kind of question. Students are much more likely to make the concept their own if asked analytical questions.

In terms of filling time, content questions take much less time to answer than analytical questions. One well-conceived analytical question can stimulate longer discussions as well as research. Learners will engage with the challenge and stay involved in the session. They are much more apt to remember content and concepts if they are actively involved in seeking responses to the questions.

Reflective questions invite learners to relate the information and concepts to their own experience. They are an essential element to "learner-centered" or "experiential" learning. The following are examples of reflective questions:

- If you were a reporter for the *Bethlehem Gazette*, what would you ask the shepherds?

- How does your family show love at Christmas?

- When is a time God surprised you?

Reflective questions enable the learner to build a bridge between the words of Scripture, the lives of biblical characters, and the events of long ago and their own experiences, feelings, values, and beliefs. The Bible comes alive when students discover that the experiences of biblical characters are much like their own. This kind of question places a value on the perspective of the learner and welcomes it. Reflective questions keep things interesting for learners.

Wonder questions awaken imagination and creative thinking. There are no right answers, and such questions may inspire ideas the leader has not even considered. The following are examples of wonder questions:

- I wonder what you would want to say to Mary and Joseph if you were in the stable.

- I wonder what your favorite Christmas memory is.

- I wonder what would happen if Jesus were born as a baby today.

Activities that allow for artistic expression, innovative action, and gratitude are good companions to wonder questions. Congregations that prefer the transmission method probably will not find a place for wonder questions in their curriculum, since right answers are so central to that method. On the other hand, congregations that value original thinking and encourage the freedom of response will enjoy the use of this type of question.

All these types of questions can be used with learners of all ages. However, expectations for response must be adapted to age characteristics. Young children love to think about wonder questions but will do so differently than middle high youth. Concrete thinkers will not be able to think conceptually as comfortably as abstract thinkers, so concepts will need to be kept very simple. As young people grow they get better and better at abstract thinking.

Life Application

Some purchased curriculums use the term "life application." This is distinct from a learner making a connection with Bible stories and his or her own life. Life application fits much better with the transmission method, in which a teacher tells students an idea or concept and then instructs them in how to apply it. The following is an example of life application.

Leader: God wants us to show love to others. We can do that by saying, "please and thank you," obeying our parents, and telling others about Jesus.

Final Steps

Publishers of purchased curriculum normally do two kinds of editing. The content editor reads for biblical and educational content. A copyeditor reads for correct language and grammar. Likewise, when your writers have completed their work, you, another qualified person, or a group of people should read through the material for consistency with the biblical material and educational theory, as well as for clarity of writing.

A copyeditor working at any publishing house follows a "style" accepted as the norm for that publisher. If you want to read for language and grammar, a variety of style books are available that represent a particular set of acceptable style practices, such as correct use of punctuation and capitalization and numerous grammar rules. A frequently used style guide is the *Chicago Manual of Style* (15th ed.; University of Chicago Press, 2006).

In materials created for use within your congregation, you may not want to spend extensive time worrying about style. On the other hand, the use of incorrect grammatical structure may result in confusing directions. If a writer uses incomplete sentences or split infinitives or incorrect verb forms, you will need to address grammatical mistakes so that the teachers will understand the directions that have been provided for them. A good basic grammar book, such as *Essentials of English* by Hopper, Gale, Foote, and Griffith (Barrons, 2000) will be helpful. Recently some books that make grammar fun, such as *When You*

Catch an Adjective, Kill It: Parts of Speech for Better and/or Worse by Ben Yagoda (Broadway Books, 2007) have become available.

Finally, you will put your curriculum in the printed or electronic format you will give to teachers. More than likely the writers have created their manuscripts using Word or WordPerfect. Certainly you can give the curriculum to teachers in this format. However, you may want to use a desktop publishing program such as Publisher to format the manuscript.

Now that you have plowed your way through all the suggestions and hand-outs, you are ready to develop your own curriculum resources. While writing your own materials is both time- and labor-intensive, the finished product will enrich and enable your educational ministry.

As a first step in developing your own materials, you may want to write out a timeline for your church. Be sure to allow time for envisioning, listening to one another, writing, and editing. Beside your timeline write the names of congregational members who can contribute to each step of the process. Set a realistic goal for finishing the first section of your work. And when you reach your goal, don't forget to celebrate!

On the next few pages you will find a complete curriculum session plan for the six-week mission study that we have been developing throughout Part 3. It will give you an idea of how a finished session in your curriculum resources can look. This sample, intended for use with fourth and fifth graders, implements the Inquiry Method.

The step-by-step process found here in Part 3 will enable you to move from your vision of educational ministry to tangible materials for fulfilling that mission. Without a doubt the journey from vision to finished product requires energy, time, and commitment. However, the fruits of the effort will be sweet and plentiful—faithful disciples, happy teachers, and the satisfaction of knowing you are working toward the goals of your ministry.

Sample Session Plan

Setting: church school

Age Group: fourth and fifth graders

Content: missions

Scope: missionary stories from Luke and Acts, historical and contemporary stories, suggestions for learners

Sequence: Jesus > coming of the Holy Spirit > events in the early church

---

Session themes and Scriptures:

    Week 1: Jesus Sends Out the Seventy (Luke 10:1-12)

    Week 2: Jesus Commissions His Followers (Luke 24:36-53)

    Week 3: The Holy Spirit Comes (Acts 2:1-13)

    Week 4: Peter and John Heal a Man (Acts 3:1-10)

    Week 5: The Baptism of the Ethiopian (Acts 8:26-40)

    Week 6: The Call of Saul (Acts 9:1-19)

Week 4

Theme: Peter and John Heal a Man

Bible Passage: Acts 3:1-10

Main Idea:
In the days following Pentecost, Peter and John were on the way to the temple to worship when they stopped to heal a man in the name of Jesus. As some of the first missionaries, Peter and John model for us the idea of sharing whatever we have with others. The man who was healed shows us the importance of responding with joy to God's good gifts.

Goal:
To hear the story of Peter and John and to think about the gifts that learners can use to share the good news with others.

Outcomes:

• Learners will be able to retell the story of Peter, John, and the lame man.

• Learners will think about the gifts they have for sharing God's love with others.

• Learners will identify a way they can share the good news with someone.

• Learners will celebrate God's love.

Opening
Open a Bible to Acts 3 and place it where the children can see it. Choose a doorway or window in your room that you can decorate as a Beautiful Gate. Have uncut tissue paper and construction paper available.

You may also have available plastic flowers, ribbons, bows, or other items that can be used to decorate the doorway.

As the children arrive greet them saying, "In the name of Jesus, I offer you a 'Good morning' and a smile." Encourage them to greet the other children as they come in, using the same expression.

Explain to the children that today's story takes place at the Beautiful Gate near the temple in Jerusalem. Tell them that they can help you make a beautiful gate here in your room. Encourage the children to begin to decorate the door or window by cutting and hanging the strips of colored paper around it. They can add the flowers, ribbons, bows, and other materials you have brought, or they can cut flower shapes from paper and add those to your beautiful gate. Be sure to welcome any other ideas the children have for decorating the doorway or window.

Supplies needed: Bible, colored tissue paper or construction paper, scissors, mounting putty, and markers. Optional: plastic flowers, ribbons, bows, other decorative items.

Presenting the Main Idea

When all the children have arrived, gather around the doorway or window you have decorated. Remind the children that last week's story told about Pentecost, the day that the church was born. Invite them to tell you anything they remember about the story. Explain that after Pentecost, those who believed in Jesus began to meet together for meals and to tell stories about Jesus. They also went to the temple to worship God and to share the good news with everyone they met.

Explain that today's story is about something that happened one day after Pentecost, when Peter and John went to the temple to pray. It took place near the Beautiful Gate in the city of Jerusalem. The story tells us about a wonderful gift that Peter and John gave to someone they met at the Beautiful Gate. Invite the children to tell you about any gifts that they have received this week. Ask questions such as:

- What are some gifts you have received this week?

- Who gave them to you?

- How did you feel when you received these gifts?

- What did you like about these gifts?

Explain that for members of the early church, sharing gifts they had with one another and with others outside the church was very important. This was a way they could show God's love.

Exploring the Main Idea

Explain to the children that this story comes from the book of Acts, and help them find Acts 3 in their Bibles. Invite them to go around the circle and read the story, with each child reading one verse. You may want to explain that *lame* is another word for being unable to walk. (Some Bible versions, including the New International Version, translate the term in Acts 3:2 as *crippled*.) When the children have finished reading, ask questions such as these to guide a discussion of the passage:

- What happened in the story?

- Why do you think the lame man was sitting at the Beautiful Gate?

- How would you feel if you had to ask people for money?

- What do you think the lame man was thinking when he first saw Peter and John? What might Peter and John have been thinking?

- Why do you think Peter and John decided to help the lame man?

- What do you want to do when you see someone who has less than you do?

- How do you think the lame man felt when he realized he could walk?

- What do you think the other people at the Beautiful Gate thought when they saw what had happened?

- What do you think happened to the lame man after he was healed?

- Imagine that you are the lame man. How would you have felt on the day *before* you were healed? How would you have felt on the day *after* you were healed?

Explain that some people like to write their feelings and personal thoughts in a journal. Pass out paper and pencils. Encourage the children to record some of the thoughts and feelings the lame man might experience, using words or drawings. When they are finished, invite the children to share what they have written or drawn in their journal.

Supplies needed: Pencils, writing paper, and markers, crayons, or colored pencils.

Responding to the Main Idea

Peter and John gave the lame man a gift. Being healed was the best gift that the man had ever received. Remind the children that God wants them to share the gifts they have just as Peter and John did. Invite the children to name some of the gifts they possess that they can give to others. As the children mention things, write them on newsprint or a white board. The children will probably begin by listing material things such as books, money, toys, etc. After you have listed these things, encourage them to think about the gifts they have to share that are not material. These gifts may be generic, such as smiles, hugs, helpfulness, or kindness. Encourage the children to also think about specific gifts they have, such as talent in singing, drawing, or playing ball. Be sure to include your own gifts in the list.

Remind the children that often we can help others by offering them a hand. Invite the children to think of things they can do to help others by using our hands. Encourage them to think of talents and skills that they can do with their hands.

Explain that they can make a card that promises someone a helping hand. Invite them to spend a minute deciding the person for whom they will make the card and what they will promise that person. Cut pieces of construction paper in half and then fold each in half. On the front of the card, have the children trace around their hands. Inside the card have them write a message to someone promising to give that person a helping hand. Encourage the children to decorate the cards using the supplies you have put out.

Have the children show one another the cards they have made with the helping hands.

Supplies needed: Construction paper, glue or glue sticks, scissors, crayons or markers. Optional: sequins, glitter, and assorted stickers.

Closing

Invite the children to tell the name of the person to whom they will give their helping hands and what they have promised to do. As the children say the names, write them on the board or newsprint.

Say a prayer thanking God for each of the people whose names you have written and for the helping hands of the children.

As the children leave, say to them, "Go out and share what you have in the name of Jesus."

Multiple Intelligences

Logical/mathematical. People who operate in this intelligence prefer numbers and abstract patterns. These learners like to play number games, use computers, debate, and solve puzzles and riddles.

Intrapersonal. People who operate in this intelligence prefer self-reflection, thinking about thinking, and spirituality. The intelligence involves the knowledge of inner feelings and emotional responses. These people enjoy independent, self-paced study, journal keeping, and individualized projects.

Musical. People who operate in this intelligence enjoy rhythmic and tonal patterns. They like to sing, listen to music, and play musical instruments. They respond to music and group singing.

Spatial. People who operate in this intelligence enjoy forming mental images and pictures in their minds. They like drawing, building, designing, and creating things, looking at pictures, and playing with machines.

Linguistic. People who operate in this intelligence use words and language effectively. They enjoy exploring ideas and concepts and express realities through words—writing, reading, talking, and listening.

Interpersonal. People who operate in this intelligence enjoy working with others. They are able to work cooperatively and have a sense of empathy for the feelings and experiences of others. They enjoy cooperative games, group brainstorming and problem solving, and interpersonal interaction.

Bodily/kinesthetic. People who operate in this intelligence enjoy using their bodies to express emotion and to articulate ideas and concepts. These people learn well through movement, touching, sports and physical games, drama, clay modeling, and project building.

Naturalist. People who operate in this intelligence are attuned to the natural world and use all their senses to enjoy the creation. They enjoy the study of nature, identifying cultural artifacts, collecting, sorting, and observing a variety of objects in nature.

Age Group Characteristics

Preschool and kindergarten children (ages 3–5) are beginning to use language to express their thoughts and experiences. They are by nature very egocentric in that they can only see their own perspective. Children this age look to external clues from others about whether something is good or bad. They are active, have short attention spans, and are concrete thinkers. Play is an important means of learning and socialization.

Younger elementary children (ages 6–9) learn best by doing, and they have very short attention spans. They think in concrete terms about things they can see, hear, taste, smell, or touch. Most cannot think about abstract ideas such as truth, love, and sin. Their faith is very literal. Since they are unable to think abstractly and like to relate to heroes, they enjoy the stories of the Bible and hearing about the people in the stories. They want to master many skills; but they still need to be cherished for themselves, not their performance. They are very active and have a very silly sense of humor.

Older elementary children (ages 10–12) have a deep need for fairness and characterize everything as right or wrong. They are beginning to question everything but do so more out of wonder than out of doubt. Their faith is very literal and reflects the faith of their parents. They are beginning to learn the fundamentals of abstract thinking. They thrive within same-gender friendships and have a strong need for same-gender role models.

Middle high youth (ages 12–14) are in the midst of a great deal of change physically, emotionally, and socially. Both boys and girls swing back and forth between adult and childlike behavior. They have a great need to be accepted and to belong, and they will do almost anything to fit in. They are developing abstract thinking skills, although many still think concretely. They need very clear boundaries that allow them a sense of freedom and that help them develop skills for responsibility. They tend to be very idealistic.

Senior high youth (ages 15–18) are forming identities separate from their families. They may question the authority of Scripture and church leaders, and they are beginning to form an understanding of faith that may be different from that of their parents. They can use abstract thinking skills and are able to think about concepts and perspectives other than their own and about the consequences of their actions. They are under tremendous pressure to succeed so that they can get into college or get a job. The longing to belong is still very strong.

PART 4

Adapting Curriculum Resources

The Challenge of Adapting Existing Curriculum

This book would not be complete without giving some attention to the process of purchasing a curriculum and adapting it for the special needs or unique setting of a particular congregation. Much of what has already been addressed in the previous section about writing your own resources also applies to the adaptation of existing curriculum materials. This chapter will introduce you to the idea of implementing that information into the challenging process of adapting a purchased curriculum.

You may be like many churches and find that curriculum resources that are published for a mass audience just miss the mark of meeting the particular needs of your congregation. The resources may not be intended for classes the size you have or for the cultural traditions of your members. You may think the materials do not include enough Bible background information or instructional guidance for your teachers. Or perhaps you like the instructional model and activities, but the theological perspective that underlies the biblical interpretation is more conservative or progressive than you are comfortable with.

The content itself may come close to what you want to teach in order to reach the goals of your educational ministry, but the materials may fall short in providing adequate interaction for learners. Maybe there isn't much attention given to creative activities or there are too few questions included to encourage discussion. Perhaps the materials do not include an emphasis on life application or address the life changes you want to promote. The curriculum may not provide opportunities for service or outreach into the wider community. Or maybe elements of the materials are just plain boring, outdated, and irrelevant.

Although the curriculum materials you have identified as the best for your congregation fall short of your goals, the idea of writing your own resources might seem overwhelming. Perhaps there are no writers in the congregation or too few people who would be willing to make a commitment to such a large and ongoing project. Within the realities of your situation, adapting a curriculum may seem like the best option. You may figure it will take only a short amount of time to make additions or adjustments that will bring the resources closer to your idea of the "perfect curriculum" for your congregation. Just add some new teaching tips or include a few creative activities, right?

Don't count on it. If you wish to have materials that truly reach your congregation's ministry goals, view of Scripture, and preference for teaching models, then adapting may be more time consuming and complicated than you anticipate. Nevertheless, it can be done and done well—*if* you apply the same step-by-step processes outlined in the previous chapters for those who decide to write their own curriculum materials *and* follow the guidelines suggested in the following chapter in which I will lead you through two processes that will make curriculum adaptation less frustrating and produce more satisfying results.

First Steps

Adapting curriculum resources begins in the same way that choosing and writing curriculum begin. First, you will need to identify the six key elements for your congregation. (Review, as needed, the worksheets and notes you generated in the workshops outlined in Part 1 of this book.) This process of naming the goals for the educational ministry of your church remains the same regardless of the form of the educational materials you ultimately provide. This important step of knowing what you want to accomplish—of knowing where you are going—is essential to any choice you make about curriculum resources.

The investment of time and energy for this process is as important for adapting curriculum as it is for writing it. Only after you have those six key elements in place will you be ready to evaluate existing curriculum materials using the process described in part 2 of this book. Keep the six key elements in focus throughout the process:

Six Key Elements

Key 1: Purpose or goal for Christian education in your church

Key 2: What the Bible is and how you use it in your educational ministry

Key 3: Settings for educational ministry in your congregation

Key 4: Content to be taught in your educational ministry

Key 5: Role of teachers in your educational ministry

Key 6: Role of learners in your educational ministry

Not many congregations start out with the goal of adapting resources for their members. You, like most other churches, will probably begin with a goal of working through the process of evaluating the available curriculum materials in order to choose one. Typically you expect to find a printed resource that is suited "as is" for your perspectives on Scripture and teaching. After all, there are so many quality resources out there! Surely you can find the perfect one to meet your needs—and that perfect curriculum will be just a phone call or mouse click away! Only as you evaluate the available resources do you discover that, as in most areas of life, there is no "perfect match" that addresses exactly the needs of your congregation. Even after your thorough and conscientious search and evaluation process, you have not found the published resource that is exactly right for your congregation.

At this point you may decide that creating a new curriculum program from scratch is more ambitious than your congregation (or Christian education department) is willing or able to undertake. So you opt to make the best of the closest match—which often means adapting it for your own needs. Many churches are already doing this—and don't even realize it. The adaptations may be ad hoc or ad lib—creative and innovative, yes, but not entirely intentional or thought through.

In the following chapter, I offer you two different processes for making the desired changes. Whether you are already adapting your purchased curriculum or considering such adaptation for the first time, you should find creative ideas and helpful strategies for implementing those ideas. You might even find useful suggestions for adapting a curriculum resource that your church wrote in years past! After all, even original materials eventually become dated as a congregation grows and changes.

Note that while some suggestions given can be used out of the context of the larger book, most of the procedures are based on the six key elements and therefore depend on users knowing what those keys are. Adapting a curriculum resource without using the previous processes will be less likely to lead to the achievement of your educational goals—especially if you do not know what those goals are. Therefore, you are encouraged to take the time and expend the energy to work through the processes given in parts 1 and 2 of this book. The results in terms of happy teachers, engaged learners, and ministry fulfillment will be well worth it.

Identifying Needs

So you have identified your six key elements. You know the goal(s) of your educational ministry, your understanding of Scripture, and your preferred teaching methods, including the role of both teachers and learners. And you have found the curriculum that comes closest to matching your overall educational needs.

However, there are some weaknesses in the curriculum and you have decided to adapt the curriculum to address those weaknesses.

The first step in adapting a curriculum resource is to state in very clear and exact terms what its weaknesses are. Unless you know what is "broken," you will be unable to fix it. Begin by looking at your six key elements and evaluating the curriculum you have chosen against those six elements.

In evaluating your chosen curriculum alongside your six key elements, it is important to know where the existing curriculum falls short of your goals and ideals. Without a clear understanding of its weaknesses, you will not be able to decide how to solve the problems or which of the two processes of adaptation (described in the following chapter) you will need to use.

These keys are foundational. A curriculum resource that falls short of your goals in those areas will make adaptation a hopelessly frustrating and ultimately futile endeavor. Therefore, it is most important to ensure that the curriculum resource shares the same *goals for educational ministry* as your church. If these goals and purposes are not the same, then no amount of adaptation will correct the problem. In the same way, if the curriculum's *view of Scripture* does not match yours, then it will be very difficult to adapt the materials for your needs. If the *role of teacher and student* conflict, you are better off writing your own materials or choosing another resource than to try to correct those differences.

If you have decided to adapt a curriculum to better meet your educational needs, the following chapter offers two different processes for adapting curriculum resources.

9 Two Strategies for Adaptation

There are two principal approaches for adapting curriculum resources so that they better match your needs and purposes. The first way involves adding to or replacing material within the curriculum, be it biblical background information for the teacher or creative activities for the learners. This is the simpler of the two methods. The second strategy is to rearrange the materials as well as adding and replacing specific features. Obviously this second approach is a much more complex and time-intensive process. Let us begin with the first.

Adapting by Adding or Replacing Material

Let's use an example and say that the curriculum you have chosen already matches your congregation's understanding of Scripture—that the Bible tells about the work of God in the words of human beings and reflects the culture of those who wrote it. One of the goals of your educational ministry is for learners to develop skills for interpretation of the Bible. However, the curriculum does not provide any background for the teachers based on critical biblical scholarship. You want to include such background information on each Scripture passage for your teachers.

Take another example. Perhaps your congregation places a high value on creative expression. The curriculum you have chosen only includes cut-and-paste activities that do not offer creative opportunities to the students. You want your Christian education program to include activities that will allow students to engage in original artwork with implements such as paint and pastels, to write poetry or music, and to respond through dramatic action. Therefore, you want to adapt the curriculum by replacing the cut-and-paste activities with additional and varied opportunities for creative expression.

In each of these cases the goal of adaptation is to provide additional or replacement resources. You can do this quite easily by copying or scanning the leader's guide and adding the desired enrichment materials. Provide specific suggestions to the teachers about how to use the background materials or mark the activity that will be replaced. You can then insert your new materials and activities in the appropriate place in the session plan.

This manner of adapting curriculum does require that someone—you or another person—write the new background material or activities. It is best to do this one to three months before the lesson will be taught. Otherwise someone—very possibly *you*—will be scrambling at the eleventh hour—Saturday night!—to get the updated lesson plans into the hands of leaders. The less lead time you provide your writers, the lower the quality and creativity the new materials will have.

If you are adding biblical background materials, for example, use the biblical exploration form and outline included in chapter 6, "Get Set" (Worksheet 10, p. 65 and Worksheet 11, p. 68). If you are adding questions or activities, review the information for writers in chapter 7, "Go," which offers guidance for writing clear directions for others to use and asking questions that engage learners' response.

Plan to spend time during teacher training workshops to explain to the teachers why the material is being changed or supplemented and to describe the format in which they will receive the adapted curriculum. If teachers are brought on board with the educational ministry goals and shown how the adaptation of the curriculum enriches that ministry, they are more apt to follow the new suggestions you are providing.

Another way to get teachers to invest in what you are doing is to invite them to write some of the new material themselves. Perhaps you have a teacher who is really good at framing questions. Invite him or her to add suggestions for additional questions in each session plan. Your pastor or seminary-trained lay leader might like to write the biblical background sections or lead a Bible study on those passages for teachers during the week. There are probably people within your congregation who are experts in a variety of creative arts and who would be willing to write or plan some activities you can include in the curriculum materials.

Don't forget that time will also need to be spent coordinating additions for different age groups and keeping track of assignments—what new material goes where and who will be writing it. Once the new sections are written, the material will need to be inserted into the correct session plan and distributed to teachers. This can be time consuming if additions are made within a lot of different age groups.

As I suggested earlier, making additions to the curriculum is the simpler and easier of the strategies for adapting existing resources to the unique needs and settings of your congregation. However, it does require working ahead in a well organized and consistent manner.

Adapting by Rearranging a Session Plan

The second method of adapting curriculum involves rearranging materials within the curriculum as well as making additions to it. Unquestionably, this approach is more time-consuming and energy-intensive than the first method. Because of the logistical factors involved, it could even take as much time as writing a curriculum from scratch.

Again, you will want to be sure that the curriculum aligns closely with the goals of the congregation. If the curriculum's content and assumptions do not, please continue the evaluation process until you find materials that do match—at least in the foundational areas highlighted on page 90. While it is certainly possible to add resources and activities and to rearrange session plans, it is not worth the effort required to transform materials so that the main goal, biblical perspectives, and teaching methods conform to your needs. It is much better stewardship of your time to choose another curriculum and adapt that to your needs.

In the first method of adapting curriculum you added background information and replaced activities. You may have also included additional questions, life applications, or service projects. However, this second method of adapting may include such things as writing your own goal and objectives, rearranging the order of the session plan, and mixing in your own additions. Like the first method, this strategy requires working ahead of a session plan—preferably three to six months ahead—so that teachers have the plans well in advance of the time when they will teach. A team of people to coordinate the efforts of writing and rearranging is equally if not more important to this method. Just one person will be overwhelmed, particularly if materials for many age groups are being adapted.

Identifying Scope and Sequence

The first step in adapting curriculum using this second method is to ascertain the scope and sequence of the content. Read chapter 5, "Get Ready," to review the issues of content, scope, and sequence. Create a Curriculum Overview (Worksheet 9, p. 57) for each quarter of material that you are considering for adaptation. In this way you can see the scope and sequence of the curriculum in one place. Then you are better equipped to make decisions about changing the sequence of the session plans.

Note again that if your concerns relate not just to the sequence of the sessions and lessons but to the overarching scope or content of the existing materials, it is probably time to consider writing your own curriculum resources rather than adapting. Changing everything will lead to as much work as writing from scratch!

Once you have determined the sequence, create a session outline (Worksheet 11, p. 68) for each session within the quarter. On each session outline, copy the theme, Bible passage, and main idea for that session. This will enable you to keep that essential information in front of you as you adapt the lesson.

Next, copy the curriculum goal and objectives for the session onto the session outline. If a goal and objectives for the session are not clearly identified within the session plan, you can rewrite the goal and objectives. See the section in "Get Set" (pp. 62–63) to review the importance of goals and outcomes and how to write them.

Considering the Session Structure

Once the main idea, the goal, and the objectives are in place, you are ready to review the structure or format of the session plan itself. Usually curriculum resources use a consistent pattern for session plans. Write the steps for the basic session structure on another piece of paper. Compare it to the structure suggested on page 64 in "Get Ready": opening, presenting the main idea, exploring the main idea, responding to the main idea, and closing. You will need to decide first whether the publisher's structure of the session is the one you want to continue to use.

At this point you have the options of renaming the sections of the structure, rearranging them, or adding sections to each session plan. For example, maybe the existing curriculum does not provide welcoming activities for leaders to use as learners arrive. You want to provide teachers with more helps for this and decide to add an opening for each session plan. Or perhaps the session does not include any opportunity for worship, and you want to add a new closing that concludes the session with worship.

Remember that the more you decide to change about the existing curriculum, the more work you are creating for yourself and the writers. In addition, extensive changes will confuse teachers and may lead to them "doing their own thing" rather than attempting to follow your convoluted revisions. At each step you will need to ascertain the amount of work involved and how you can make the critical changes in as simple and straightforward a way as possible.

Once you have identified the structure you want to use, change the headings on the session outline. I would encourage you to use the computer for this process so that you can insert the headings into the session outline easily. Then you can input the new activities or the name of existing activities from the curriculum. For reasons of copyright (see discussion following) you are discouraged from transferring or copying even an edited version of the instructions from the existing curriculum into your revised session plan.

Evaluating Session Activities

Now you are ready to begin the process of evaluating each activity and deciding what you want to use and where changes or additions need to be made. This is a time-consuming process. You will need to decide whether to do this yourself or to invite a group of people to share the responsibility. I recommend the team approach, especially if you have gone through the important process of establishing your congregation's six key elements. With that shared understanding, as well as clear identification of the goal and objectives for the session, everyone on the team will be using the same standards for evaluation.

Once the needs for additions or replacements are identified, you can pass the session outlines into the hands of writers to complete the plan for each session. Please remember that all of this takes time and that you need to be working at least three to six months in advance of the Sunday that the session plan will be used.

Word needs to be added here about copyright issues. Every curriculum that you purchase has gone through a process of design, writing, and editing, and it has been copyrighted by the publisher. Do not disregard the work of writers and editors or federal copyright laws when you adapt curriculum. That means that you cannot copy the words of the curriculum into another document without crediting the passage. And certainly it means you cannot copy the material into another document, edit it, and call it your own. Respect the time and creative skills and insights of writers by noting proper credit on your version, something to the effect of "This curriculum resource has been adapted from TITLE, published by PUBLISHER (QUARTER, YEAR) for use by YOUR CHURCH NAME, ADDRESS."

Challenges of Adapting Curriculum

As suggested throughout this section, there are many challenges involved in the decision to adapt curriculum. It is important to make the decision to adapt with full recognition and acknowledgment of these challenges. A quick decision to buy the best match and adapt it can lead to unexpected demands on the time and energy of one or more individuals. Therefore the decision needs to be well informed and carefully considered.

Who?

The first challenge of adapting curriculum is the question of who will do it. A congregation that employs a full-time educator may assume that the educator can do the work easily in the time that is already available. After all, that person is trained and prepared to create curriculum resources! First, congregations should not assume that their educator has the skills for curriculum writing. Not all Christian educators are trained in creating curriculum materials, just as not all pianists are trained in (or talented at) musical composition. Second, such congregations need to be aware that curriculum writing, whether in brief for adaptation or at length in creating a new resource, is time-consuming. Any educator who agrees to this effort will use time to write that he or she is currently using in other ways. The congregation will have to understand that the new task will require a trade-off in other responsibilities.

The project of adapting a curriculum is best done by a *group* of people with a *variety* of skills. Some need the ability to evaluate the educational process; some need to be able to write skillfully and clearly for teachers and varying age-levels; some need to be competent organizers who can distribute the session revisions; others need the skills to train teachers to use the new session plans. Unless a congregation is willing to make a commitment to long-range efforts, they are better off doing the best they can with an existing curriculum.

How?

Another challenge is the issue of how to create an adapted resource that teachers can actually use. How will you make your changes and additions in a way that the adapted material is easy to understand and simple to follow? Adding biblical background material is a worthy adaptation, but not if the new text is too scholarly for the average teacher to comprehend. Supplementing cut-and-paste crafts with more creative and elaborate activities is a wonderful idea, but not if the instructions are incoherent, the budget doesn't cover the supplies, or a specialized skill is needed for successful implementation.

If teachers do not have material they can make sense of and use without excessive effort, they simply will not use the material. They will create their own or use the curriculum "as is" rather than make use of the revisions that someone else spent time and energy preparing. Your adaptations must be teacher-friendly or they will not be used.

When?

A third major challenge facing those who adapt existing curriculum is time. Having enough time is a challenge facing all of us in today's busy world. The decision to adapt needs a reality check. Can you evaluate the existing resources, identify the weaknesses, and plan for the adaptation at least six months in advance? Can you schedule teacher training before the quarter begins to orient the teachers to the new or newly adapted materials? Can the revisions and additions be completed two to three months in advance of the Sunday they will be used? How complicated are the revised sessions? Will the teachers have sufficient time to prepare the revised lessons from week to week? If the answer to one or more of these questions is no or even maybe, another plan is probably needed.

Why?

This question leads us to another one. Why take all the time and energy required to adapt an existing curriculum? Is it worth the investment from your Christian education team? Is it worth the trade-off in time the educator may spend writing when he or she could be working with teachers or relating to learners? What is most important here? The answers to those questions may be the ones that best guide you in your decision to adapt—and the specific kind of adaptations you choose.

This is, perhaps, the key question: What difference will a proposed change in the curriculum make to the faith of learners? If you cannot provide a strong argument that adapting the material will lead to stronger faith and more loving disciples, then leave the curriculum alone. Your time may be much better invested in relating to the individuals who are leaders and learners than it is sitting at a computer writing activities someone may or may not use.

In Summary

The purpose of this section has been to guide you in deciding whether or not to purchase an existing curriculum and then adapt it to be a more perfect match for your church's educational goals. It has sought to identify the challenges of adapting curriculum as well as providing suggestions for how to go about the process. Whatever you decide, adaptations need to be grounded in the six key elements of your congregation's Christian education ministry and in an evaluation process that makes use of the congregational priorities and goals identified within these elements.

Of the two processes for adapting curriculum described here, the one requiring the least amount of extra writing and most promise for improving a session plan is the first one. Inserting biblical background material and adding questions, creative activities, life application, or mission projects can strengthen the best-matching curriculum. When congregations get into the tasks required by the second method, they may want to stop and ascertain whether choosing another curriculum or writing their own will lead to more satisfactory results.

Conclusion

I complete the writing of this book filled with a great sense of hope and excitement and appreciation. During this writing process I have had an opportunity to share portions of it with friends of mine who are Christian educators. They have been affirming and excited about the possibilities the book offers for helping congregations in the never-ending search for curriculum materials.

It is my hope that you as the reader are equally filled with hope and excitement after reading the book. I wish we could sit down and talk about what you have found helpful and the questions you have. Although there is a great deal of material contained in these pages, I hope that the format of the book makes it easy for you to access the information that you need.

I have made every effort to provide step-by-step guidelines that are clear and meet the goal of being easy to use. I trust that these guidelines will give structure and direction to your educational ministry efforts.

For the last ten years I have been using the six key elements to guide my own curriculum writing and teaching. I cannot urge you strongly enough to take the time to identify the key elements for your congregation before attempting to review, choose, develop, or adapt curriculum. Those elements are a helpful guide for unlocking the mysteries of choosing curriculum resources for any congregation. Of the six key elements, the most important is to articulate the purpose of Christian education in your church. Without a clear understanding of that goal you will find decisions about your church's curriculum to be difficult and frustrating.

The purpose of this book is to assist you in choosing or developing curriculum resources so that you can reach your educational ministry goals, but those print or media materials are only one element in your church's Christian education curriculum. They are not an end in themselves but a means to equip your congregation to share the gospel. Thus the identification of curriculum materials is ultimately part of a strategy for reaching the broader ministry goals of your congregation and of Christ's church universal.

What's more, I hope you remember that your curriculum materials are tools—and like any other tools, they are only as useful as the person who handles them. So, after you have chosen or written the "just-right" curriculum, entrust them to your teachers and support those teachers in using the curriculum effectively. Teachers are the most important component of your educational ministry. They are the ones who bring their love for God and Christ's church to the children, youth, and adult learners in your congregation.

The curriculum materials are only an aid for teachers to use. It is teachers' relationship with Christ and their relationship with learners that best teaches the ways of faith. Along with developing and choosing your curriculum, plan a way to introduce the curriculum to your teachers. The training of teachers needs to include not only the resources themselves but background for the Bible passages, innovative teaching methods, and insight into the learning styles of students.

Don't forget to explain to teachers the process the committee used in making its curriculum choice. It is important that teachers know the purpose of educational ministry in your congregation and understand how what they do contributes to that goal. Show the teachers a copy of your six key elements and review each element with them. It may even be a good idea to review the elements with prospective teachers so that they will know what the congregation believes.

It is my hope that your sense of what is possible in Christian education has grown and that your imagination is ready to take flight. Rather than approaching curriculum planning as a chore, may you experience freedom in identifying or creating the "just-right" curriculum for your congregation.

May God go with you on this journey and fill you with the insights and commitment needed for the task of evaluating, choosing, developing or adapting curriculum resources for your congregation. I pray that your educational ministry will bear much fruit.

APPENDIX A

Bible Study Resources

Study Bibles

Every curriculum writer should have access to a study Bible that includes a complete version of one translation of the Bible (Old and New Testaments) with commentary, word studies, cross references, and maps.

The Original African American Heritage Study Bible. Cain Hope Felder, ed. Valley Forge, Pa.: Judson Press, 2006.

The Harper Collins Study Bible, Fully Revised and Updated. New Revised Standard Version. With concordance; including apocryphal deuterocanonical books. Harold W. Attridge, ed. New York: HarperOne, 2006.

Life Application Study Bible (NLT). Carol Stream, IL: Tyndale House, 2004. Various translations and editions available, including NKJV, NIV, large print, and student edition.

Nelson's NKJV Study Bible. Nashville: Thomas Nelson, 2005.

The New Interpreter's Study Bible: New Revised Standard Version with Apocrypha. Walter J. Harrelson, ed. Nashville: Abingdon Press, 2003.

Zondervan NIV Study Bible, Revised Edition. Grand Rapids: Zondervan, 2002.

Concise Concordance (includes the majority of key words of the Bible with their primary appearances)

Kohlenberger, John R. III, ed. *The Concise Concordance to the New Revised Standard Version.* Oxford: Oxford University Press, 1996.

Complete Concordance (includes all the key words of the Bible with all of their appearances)

Strong, John. *New Strong's Exhaustive Concordance.* Nashville: Nelson, 2003.

Bible Dictionary (includes brief articles, illustrations, and biblical references on biblical books, places, people, and concepts that provide basic information; articles are arranged alphabetically)

Pilch, John J. *The Cultural Dictionary of the Bible*. Collegeville, MN: Liturgical Press, 1999.

The HarperCollins Bible Dictionary. Paul J. Achtemeier, gen. ed. San Francisco: HarperSanFrancisco, 1996.

Buttrick, George A., et al. *The Interpreter's Dictionary of the Bible*. Nashville: Abingdon, 1962–76. (This set includes four volumes and a supplementary volume.)

Bible Commentaries (provide comments on the background and meaning of each passage of the Bible)

Harper's Bible Commentary. James L. Mays, gen. ed. San Francisco: Harper & Row, 1988.

Albright, William F., and David Noel Freedman, gen. eds. *The Anchor Bible*. Garden City, NY: Doubleday, 1964 –.

Alexander, Neil M., gen. ed. *The New Interpreter's Bible*. Nashville: Abingdon, 1994–.

Mays, James L., series ed. *Interpretation: A Bible Commentary for Teaching and Preaching*. Louisville: John Knox, 1982–.

Bible Atlas (helps locate persons and events in their proper time and place; combines geography and history by using maps, pictures, and narrative to tell the biblical story in the sequence in which it happened)

Brisco, Thomas V. Holman *Bible Atlas*. Nashville: Broadman and Holman, 1999.

Curtis, Adrian. *Oxford Bible Altas*. Oxford: Oxford University Press, 2007.

Dowley, Tim. *The Student Atlas*. Minneapolis: Augsburg Fortress, 2005.

Curriculum Resource Publishers

The publishers and organizations listed here all produce traditional, quarterly Sunday school materials. This list is not intended to be all inclusive, nor does it represent an endorsement of the products offered by each publisher.

Abingdon Press
201 8th Avenue S
PO Box 801
Nashville, TN 37202-0801
www.abingdonpress.com
800-251-3320

Accent Publications
4050 Lee Vance View
Colorado Springs, CO 80918
www.davidccook.com
800-323-7543

Augsburg Fortress
PO Box 1209
Minneapolis, MN 55440-1209
www.augsburgfortress.com
800-328-4648

Brethren Press
1451 Dundee Ave
Elgin, IL 60120
www.brethrenpress.com
800-441-3712

David C. Cook
4050 Lee Vance View
Colorado Springs, CO 80918
www.davidccook.com
800-323-7543

Discipleland
2643 Midpoint Dr
Fort Collins, CO 80525-4428
www.discipleland.com
866-343-2475

Faith Alive Christian Resources
2850 Kalamazoo Ave SE
Grand Rapids, MI 49560
www.faithaliveresources.org
800-333-8300

Godprints
4050 Lee Vance View
Colorado Springs, CO 80918
www.davidccook.com
800-323-7543

Gospel Light
1957 Eastman Ave
Ventura, CA 93003
www.gospellight.com
800-4-GOSPEL

Group Publishing
PO Box 481
Loveland, CO 80539
www.grouppublishing.com
800-447-1070

Judson Press
PO Box 851
Valley Forge, PA 19482-0851
www.judsonpress.com
800-458-3766

LifeWay Christian Resources
One LifeWay Plaza
Nashville, TN 37234
www.lifeway.com
800-458-2772

Mennonite Publishing Network
616 Walnut Ave
Scottdale, PA 15683
www.mph.org
800-245-7894

Regular Baptist Press
1300 North Meacham Rd
Schaumburg, IL 60173-4806
www.rbpstore.org
888.588.1600

Scripture Press
4050 Lee Vance View
Colorado Springs, CO 80918
www.davidccook.com
800-323-7543

Standard Publishing
8805 Governor's Hill Dr Ste 400
Cincinnati, OH 45249
www.standardpub.com
800-543-1353

Union Gospel Press
PO Box 6059
Cleveland, OH 44101
www.uniongospelpress.com
216-749-2100

United Methodist Publishing House
201 8th Ave S
PO Box 801
Nashville, TN 37202-0801
www.umph.org
800-672-1789

Urban Ministries, Inc.
1551 Regency Ct
Calumet City, IL 60409
www.urbanministries.com
800-860-8642